T0278093

CONFUSED

by the

ODDS

Also by
David Lockwood

Fooled by the Winners:
How Survivor Bias Deceives Us

Outplayed:
How Game Theory Is Used Against Us

CONFUSED

by the

ODDS

How Probability Misleads Us

DAVID LOCKWOOD

GREENLEAF
BOOK GROUP PRESS

Published by Greenleaf Book Group Press
Austin, Texas
www.gbgpress.com

Copyright © 2023 David Lockwood

All rights reserved.

Thank you for purchasing an authorized edition of this book and for
complying with copyright law. No part of this book may be reproduced,
stored in a retrieval system, or transmitted by any means, electronic,
mechanical, photocopying, recording, or otherwise, without written
permission from the copyright holder.

Distributed by Greenleaf Book Group

For ordering information or special discounts for bulk purchases, please
contact Greenleaf Book Group at PO Box 91869, Austin, TX 78709,
512.891.6100.

Design and composition by Greenleaf Book Group
Cover design by Greenleaf Book Group
Cover Image: ©iStockphoto/mrgao and ©iStockphoto/Nerthuz

Publisher's Cataloging-in-Publication data is available.

Print ISBN: 979-8-88645-003-3

eBook ISBN: 979-8-88645-004-0

Part of the Tree Neutral® program, which offsets the number of trees
consumed in the production and printing of this book by taking proactive
steps, such as planting trees in direct proportion to the number of trees
used: www.treeneutral.com

TreeNeutral

Printed in the United States of America on acid-free paper

22 23 24 25 26 27 28 29   10 9 8 7 6 5 4 3 2 1

First Edition

To my family

"I know too well that these arguments from probabilities are imposters, and unless great caution is observed in the use of them, they are apt to be deceptive."

—PLATO, *Phaedo*

"Doctors say that Nordberg has a 50–50 chance of living, though there's only a 10 percent chance of that."

—POLICE CAPTAIN ED HOCKEN, played by George Kennedy in the movie *The Naked Gun: From the Files of Police Squad!*

CONTENTS

COVID-19 and Coins

Medical Tests: Don't Panic

After an annual physical, you receive an unexpected call from the doctor.

"You tested positive for the coronavirus," she says.

You are surprised. Only one in one hundred individuals in the local community are infected. But the doctor states that the test is 90 percent accurate. In other words, if you have the coronavirus, there is a 90 percent chance you will test positive, and if you do not have the virus, there is a 90 percent chance you will test negative.

Your heart sinks.

But then the doctor calmly states, "Don't panic. There is only an 8 percent chance you have COVID-19."[1]

She is correct. You have been misled by probability.

Probability

Probability is the branch of mathematics that tells us the odds something could happen. It helps us understand the past and predict the future.

We do not have a perfect knowledge of the world around us and how it works, so uncertainty is a basic part of the human experience. In the case of COVID-19, a positive test result does not necessarily mean you are infected. Because we do not understand all there is to know about COVID-19, medical tests yield probabilities, not certainties. In fact, we cannot even predict the outcome of a simple coin toss. We don't know enough about the exact twitches of muscles in the hand, the air currents in the room, the irregularities on the surface of the table, etc., to determine whether the result will be heads or tails.

It is sometimes possible for us to have good intuition about the odds of a particular outcome. For example, we know that a fair coin thrown into the air is about equally likely to land on either side. But we often do not have good intuition about how uncertainty impacts much of modern life. Hundreds of thousands of years of *Homo sapiens* evolution did not equip us with brains capable of easily computing the odds that we are infected with the coronavirus, given a positive test result. Until recently, this ability was not important to having more kids.

In fields as diverse as investments (expected financial returns), criminal justice (DNA evidence), science (randomized controlled experiments), and military strategy (nuclear war), probability can mislead us. In today's world, we are frequently confused by the odds.

About This Book

Many books have been published on probability, but most are laden with row after row of formulas and proofs. No such mathematical expressions are to be found here. This book presents a series of examples that illustrate how the mathematics of probability can be used to solve real-world problems. This book is about application, not theory.

We start with games involving dice and the gambler's fallacy, then examine the Monty Hall and two-child problems before moving on to real-world examples, such as falsely convicting innocent mothers of murdering their children. We discuss normal distributions and how fat tails disrupt our models of financial returns for stocks and bitcoins, income and wealth inequality, and estimates of battle deaths from global wars in the future. We then turn to the limitations of induction to determine whether reports of miracles are credible (the reason some have faith in God) and whether conclusions from randomized controlled experiments are reliable (the reason many have faith in science). Next, we explain Bayes' theorem and show how this powerful tool has been used by the US military to locate sunken submarines and by billions of email users to block unwanted messages. We demonstrate how causal diagrams can untangle cause and effect in a wide variety of subjects, such as the role of genetics in intelligence and racial bias in policing. Last, we apply Bayes' theorem and causal diagrams to the political polarization of the American electorate and COVID-19.

We begin in sixteenth-century Italy with the founder of the theory of probability. In addition to being a first-rate doctor and mathematician, this person was a well-respected and highly compensated astrologer.

But his career as a physician, math professor, and fortune teller came to an abrupt end after he cast the horoscope of Jesus Christ and was jailed by the Inquisition.

CHAPTER 1

The Odds: Not What You Think

Girolamo Cardano: The Founder of Probability and Bad Luck

Girolamo Cardano (1501–1576) was an Italian mathematician, physician, astronomer, astrologer, and professional gambler.[1] He was the first to propose a system for the use of negative integers and to suggest the existence of imaginary numbers. Cardano was one of the most important mathematicians of his age and wrote the first known treatise on probability.

Cardano was the son of Fazio Cardano and a young woman named Chiara Micheri. Fazio did not marry Micheri until the last days of his life, many years after Cardano was born. Fazio was a close friend of Leonardo da Vinci, who frequently consulted with Fazio on questions about geometry. Cardano reports in his autobiography that he entered this world despite several repeated attempts by his mother to abort the pregnancy by ingesting poisons. He claimed this accounted for the various ailments that plagued him throughout his life—kidney trouble, heart palpitations, an infected nipple, a cleft chin, a pronounced stutter, only fourteen good teeth, and periodic impotence.

As the child of an unmarried mother, Cardano grew up poor but supported himself through gambling. He was by all accounts a brilliant student at the University of Padua and graduated with a medical degree in 1526. He applied for admission to the College of Physicians in Milan but was rejected due to his out-of-wedlock birth. Unable to find work in Milan, Cardano set himself up as a country doctor in Sacco, a small village outside Padua.

In Sacco, Cardano married but couldn't support his family as a doctor and eventually moved with his wife and children back to Milan. As a young boy, he had been acquainted with many of his father's friends, including da Vinci, and was able to obtain a job as a public lecturer at the Piatti Foundation, a school set up for the instruction of poor youths. With a steady source of income, Cardano devoted his time to research and writing, and published a series of popular texts on medicine, mathematics, and science. He also treated some wealthy patients to supplement his earnings. Because he was not licensed, this earned him the disdain of local doctors.

In response to being snubbed by his fellow physicians, Cardano published a short book in 1536, *On the Bad Practices of Medicine in Common Use*, in which he wrote the following passage: "The things that give most reputation to a physician nowadays are his manners, servants, carriage, clothes, smartness, and caginess, all displayed in a sort of artificial and insipid way; learning and experience seem to count for nothing."[2]

Cardano's book caused a public scandal in Milan, and he was called before the board of physicians. Fortunately, he had previously healed and befriended several influential businessmen and leaders of the Roman Catholic Church, and the board of physicians was forced to amend its constitution to allow children born out of wedlock to become members. In 1539, Cardano was duly voted in as a member.

Within a few years, Cardano was the most prominent physician in Milan. Over the next decade, his reputation as a physician spread throughout Italy and Europe. His income soared—largely from widely read books on medicine and consultation fees from the rich and powerful. During this period, Cardano also wrote a series of books on his philosophy of life that were reprinted throughout Europe. Cardano's *Consolation* was translated into English in 1573 and is believed to have been read by Shakespeare.[3] Some scholars believe that Hamlet is reading from *Consolation* when he enters the stage holding a book and says, "To be, or not to be . . . For in that sleep of death what dreams may come, when we have shuffled off this mortal coil . . ."[4] Cardano's *Consolation* contains a similar passage.[5]

Cardano also wrote the first popular modern science books on record, which were among the best-selling books of the late sixteenth century, a time when the Renaissance and new methods of inquiry were sweeping across Western Europe. However, Cardano's popularity as a writer seems to have exceeded his popularity as a person. In his autobiography, Cardano described himself as "hot tempered, single-minded, and given to women . . . cunning, crafty, sarcastic, diligent, impertinent, sad, treacherous, magician and sorcerer, miserable, hateful, lascivious, lying, obsequious."[6] He was also a highly skilled but compulsive gambler and lost several fortunes during his lifetime. And he likely plagiarized one of his most well-known texts on algebra, which provided a partial solution to cubic equations.

Cardano could also be considered one of the founders of bad

luck. His wife died in 1546 while their children were still young. His daughter, after allegedly seducing her brother Giovanni, became pregnant and undertook an abortion that left her sterile. After the affair with his sister, Giovanni married. His new wife proceeded to cheat on him openly. She gave birth to three boys in succession, all of whom were the offspring of her lovers. The couple fought frequently and violently. After one of these fights, Giovanni unsuccessfully attempted to poison his unfaithful wife. He was arrested, and Cardano himself led the defense of his son at trial. But Giovanni was convicted, sentenced to death, and beheaded. He was just twenty-six years old. Cardano was devastated by the loss of his son and the public humiliation. He was forced to resign his teaching positions and lost most of his patients.

In 1562, a powerful friend, the Archbishop of Milan, whose mother's serious illness had been cured by Cardano, arranged for Cardano to be appointed as a professor of medicine at the University of Bologna. Cardano jumped at the chance to begin a new life in a new town. But Cardano was not thrilled that another son, Aldo, chose to relocate to Bologna with him. Aldo had lost large amounts of his father's money gambling and previously had spent several years in Italian jails for various crimes. In Bologna, Aldo resumed his gambling and criminal activities. This culminated in 1569 when Aldo burglarized his father's house and took large sums of money and jewels. Cardano reported the theft to the police, and Aldo was once again behind bars.

Less than a year later, on October 6, 1570, Cardano was arrested without warning and imprisoned on a charge of heresy. Some suspect that Aldo had denounced his father to the Inquisition. Others believe his popular writings had caught the attention of the orthodox Pope Pius V, a fervent believer in the Counter-Reformation movement. In addition to his income from books and medicine, Cardano earned commissions from drawing horoscopes for the rich and famous. To further his reputation in this line of business, Cardano published the horoscope of Jesus Christ and suggested that the events in the life on earth of the Son of God were the product of astrological forces. Cardano insisted that the star of Bethlehem over the Child's manger on Christmas Eve was just a well-known comet and not due to the workings of a Divine Hand in the night sky.[7] Cardano was jailed for three months and then released under house arrest. There is no record of his trial before the inquisitor of Como, and curiously, Cardano never refers to it in his autobiography. Cardano was eventually freed but was prohibited from lecturing or publishing books. Cardano died in 1576, close to his seventy-fifth birthday.[8]

After his death, some claimed Cardano had poisoned himself.[9] The story was that he had cast his own horoscope, predicting the day of his death, and when the date arrived and he was still in good health, he committed suicide because he could not tolerate the public humiliation of being wrong.

Over a century later, the mathematician and philosopher Gottfried Leibniz wrote, "Cardano was a great man with all his faults; without them he would have been incomparable."[10]

Cardano the Gambler: Math for Profit

As a youth, Cardano supported himself through gambling. He was also an expert at chess, which was typically played for money during the Renaissance.[11]

In his autobiography, Cardano wrote that he abandoned his medical practice and research for long periods to gamble:

> *I fell into the habit of going every day to the house of Antonio Vimercati, a noble in our town, for the purpose of playing chess. We played for stakes from one to two reals a game, and since I won*

constantly, I could take home every single day about one gold piece . . . but through this habit I had fallen so low, that for two years and some months, I neglected my medical practice, my other incomes, my reputation and my studies.[12]

In addition to regularly playing chess, Cardano carefully studied table games and other games of chance. In *The Book on Games of Chance*, he set out three fundamental principles that would come to form the basis of modern probability theory. His interest in the subject was not academic—this short book is basically a gambler's guide to winning and contains practical advice, such as strategies for bluffing, how to spot marked cards and crooked dice, and admonitions not to play when tired or drunk. However, in the last chapters of this first book on probability, Cardano became the first to write about a method for expressing probabilities in terms of a ratio of favorable to total outcomes. Cardano laid out a two-step process: 1) determine the number of total possible outcomes, which he labeled the "circuit" and today we call the sample space, and 2) divide that number by the number of favorable outcomes.

For example, in the case of the throw of a pair of dice, the sample space has thirty-six possible outcomes, as represented below:

(1,1) (1,2) (1,3) (1,4) (1,5) (1,6) (2,1) (2,2) (2,3)
(2,4) (2,5) (2,6) (3,1) (3,2) (3,3) (3,4) (3,5) (3,6)
(4,1) (4,2) (4,3) (4,4) (4,5) (4,6) (5,1) (5,2) (5,3)
(5,4) (5,5) (5,6) (6,1) (6,2) (6,3) (6,4) (6,5) (6,6)

To calculate the probability of two ones, we count the number of favorable outcomes in the sample space (1) and divide that by the number of possible outcomes (36). That yields a probability of two ones in a roll of two dice to be 1:36.

This two-step process seems like common sense to modern readers. But no one had previously expressed the idea of probability as the ratio of favorable to total outcomes within a sample space. Previous discussions of games of chance offered rules of thumb based on observed outcomes from past experience. For the first time, Cardano put forward a general method to calculate probabilities in any game or situation based on the idea that the likelihood of a given outcome can be quantified, independent of past experience. Cardano's method of constructing a sample space and then adding up potential outcomes enables us to avoid being misled by probability.

A good example of the use of Cardano's method is a question concerning a popular television game show during the 1960s.

The Monty Hall Problem: To Switch or Not to Switch

On September 9, 1990, *Parade* magazine published a question from Craig Whitaker of Columbia, Maryland, in the periodical's "Ask Marilyn" column. Whitaker posed a question about the best strategy for a game show in which the contestant was shown three doors. Goats were behind two of the doors, and a car was behind the third. He wrote:

> *You pick a door, say No. 1, and the host, who knows what's behind the doors, opens another door, say No. 3, which has a goat. He then says to you: "Do you want to pick door No. 2?" Is it to your advantage to switch your choice?*[13]

Mr. Whitaker was referring to the popular TV game show *Let's Make a Deal*, which aired from 1963 to 1976 and then again from 1980 to 1991, totaling more than 4,500 episodes.[14] The initial run of the show was hosted by the amiable Monty Hall, assisted by the provocatively clad Carol Merrill, Miss California of 1957. After a contestant picked a door, Monty would point to one of the remaining two doors and Carol would reveal a "zonk," a prize of minimal value, often a goat. Zonks were concealed behind two of the three stage doors.

The writer of the "Ask Marilyn" column was Marilyn vos Savant.[15] Born in St. Louis, Missouri, in 1946, vos Savant was identified as a prodigy as a child. She married at sixteen, had two children, and divorced in her twenties. She married again, but the second marriage ended several years later, and in 1983 she moved to New York City to become a writer. In 1985, based on her score of 228 on an intelligence quotient test, vos Savant was identified by Guinness World Records as the smartest person alive. With her newfound notoriety, vos Savant was hired by *Parade* to write the "Ask Marilyn" column, which she has continued to pen to the present day.

In her 1990 column, vos Savant answered Mr. Whitaker's question in the affirmative: it is always an advantage to switch.

Immediately, letters began pouring in. In the following months, more than ten thousand letters were received by *Parade*, some from PhDs in math and the sciences.[16] Over 90 percent of the letters argued that vos Savant was wrong.[17]

Scott Smith, a PhD in math, wrote in with these chastising words: "You blew it, and you blew it big! Since you seem to have difficulty grasping the basic principle at work here, I'll explain." Confidently erroneous, he scolded vos Savant: "There is enough mathematical illiteracy in this country, and we don't need the world's highest IQ propagating more. Shame!"[18] Others were more direct. One reader wrote simply, "You are the goat!"[19] Another male reader stated, "I am in shock that after being corrected by at least three mathematicians, you still do not see your mistake."[20] A third male reader cautioned, "Maybe women look at math problems differently than men."[21]

Vos Savant's critics reasoned as follows: Let's say the contestant picked Door 1. Once the host revealed the goat behind Door 2, then the prize was either behind Door 1 or Door 3. Since only two possibilities remain, the chances the prize is behind one of the two remaining doors is 50:50. Therefore, there is no advantage in switching. (You can repeat this with the contestant initially picking Door 2 or 3 and the same logic applies.)

But vos Savant was right.

Let's construct the sample space using Cardano's method. Let's assign P and G to represent the prize and goat, respectively. The possible locations of the prize and goats are PGG, GPG, and GGP for Doors 1, 2, and 3, respectively.

Assume a contestant picks Door 1, and then the host opens one of the other doors to reveal a goat. If the contestant does not switch, then there is a 1:3 chance they get the prize (PGG) and a 2:3 likelihood they get the goat (GPG, GGP). Therefore, the contestant should always switch. The same reasoning applies if they initially pick Door 2 or 3.

Vos Savant in her column did not set out a sample space but clearly stated the problem. To start off, when a contestant first chooses one of the three doors, the odds are 1:3 that the prize is behind that door and 2:3 that the prize is behind one of the other two doors. After making their choice, the contestant is given more information. The host opens one of the other doors—but the host only opens a door that doesn't have a prize behind it. Vos Savant wrote, "So, when you switch, you win if the prize is behind #2 or #3. You win either way! But if you don't switch, you win only if the prize is behind door #1.[22]

If this is not convincing, then imagine there are one hundred doors behind which are one prize and ninety-nine goats. The contestant picks Door 1. The host then opens Doors 2 to 99, revealing ninety-eight goats. After the host opens ninety-eight doors containing a barnyard animal, the odds the prize is behind Door 1 are still 1:100. But the odds the prize is behind Door 100 have now increased to 99:100.

On the actual show, the "deals" offered by Monty were less straightforward. After all, everyone would switch if the game were laid out as clearly as it was in Mr. Whitaker's question. Even if contestants were confused by chance, after hundreds of shows it would be crystal clear based on observed outcomes that it was better to switch. Television viewers would quickly become bored with hour after hour of switching by contestants.

As Hall reported years later in an interview, he always knew which of the two remaining doors held the goat but did not always pick that door and offer the contestant the choice to switch. He also frequently offered contestants varying amounts of money not to switch. A contestant might surmise that if Hall offered money not to switch that switching was better. But Hall said these offers of cash not to switch were frequently bluffs to keep contestants guessing. Contestants on *Let's Make a Deal* were in effect playing poker with Hall, and he held all the cards. Unless a contestant could read Hall for "tells," then there was no reason to switch, as the actions of the host did not provide reliable information.

As a result, on *Let's Make a Deal*, there was, in fact, no clear advantage in switching, and some criticized vos Savant on this basis. But she did not opine on *Let's Make a Deal*. She responded to a specific question by her reader.

Her answer was correct.

Another example of using Cardano's method for calculating probabilities relates to siblings.

The Two-Child Problem: The Missing Brother

In the October 1959 edition of *Scientific American*, Martin Gardner featured in his "Mathematical Games" column what he called "the two children problem." Gardner, who died in 2010 at the age of ninety-five, was a prolific author. He published more than one hundred books and has been credited, more than any other writer, with introducing the general public to mathematics.[23]

Gardner set out the two-child problem in the form of a question: Mr. Smith has two children. At least one of them is a boy. What is the probability that both children are boys?[24]

Let's call this Question 1, or Q1. Many reason that the probability that both children are boys in Q1 is 1:2, since Mr. Smith's other child is equally likely to be a boy or a girl. But this is an example of how we are misled by probability.

Using Cardano's method, let's define the sample space. There are four possible combinations of boys and girls. In this sample space, a capital letter corresponds to the older child.

Bb, Bg, Gb, Gg

We can eliminate Gg, because at least one of Mr. Smith's children is a boy. That leaves three other possibilities: Bb, Bg, or Gb. Therefore, the probability that Mr. Smith has two boys is 1:3.

What if we are also told that the boy is the older child, and we are then asked whether that changes the probability that Mr. Smith has two boys? Let's call this Q2. Many would intuit that this additional restrictive condition decreases the odds that both children are boys. In fact, it does the opposite.

If Mr. Smith's son is older, then we can eliminate not only Gg but also Gb. That leaves Bb and Bg. Hence, the probability that Mr. Smith has two boys, one of whom is older, is 1:2. The fact that one of the boys is older increases the chances that both are boys. To most, this is counterintuitive.

Even more perplexing is the situation in which we bump into

Mr. Smith on the street, and he says, "I have two children, one of whom is the boy standing next to me." Let's call this Q3. In Q1, we are told one of his children is a boy. In Q3, we visually verify this. The fact that Mr. Smith is standing next to a son would not seem to change the odds that he has two boys, and many deduce that the odds that both are boys are no different from those for Q1, or 1:3.

But that is not true.

Let's define the sample space. Mr. Smith could have elected not to take the son at his side for a walk. Or the boy next to Mr. Smith could have stayed home. In either of these cases, there are eight different combinations of sons and daughters, four in which his son came for a walk and four in which he did not. A bold letter indicates a child who came for a walk with their father:

Bb Bg Gb Gg
Bb Bg Gb Gg

We can eliminate **Gb, Gg, Bg,** and Gg because those are examples of a girl walking with her father. That leaves four possibilities out of a total of eight. If Mr. Smith is standing next to his son, then the odds he has two boys is 1:2. The fact that we see Mr. Smith's son and are not just told he exists has increased the chances that Mr. Smith has two boys from 1:3 in Q1 to 1:2 in Q3.

In addition to the idea of constructing sample spaces to calculate odds, Cardano was the first to propose the "multiplication rule." Cardano wrote that the probability of two or more independent events occurring jointly or simultaneously should be calculated by multiplying the probabilities of each event. Although this may seem intuitive, we are still confused by the odds when we fail to follow Cardano's power rule.

Dice: The Odds Are Less Than You Think

To illustrate Cardano's multiplication rule, consider the throw of two fair dice. What are the chances of two sixes?[25] Since the chance of a one from a roll of a single die is 1:6, some believe the likelihood of two sixes from two dice is 1:6 + 1:6, or 1:3.

But the roll of two dice comprises two independent rolls of a single die. Cardano stated that we should multiply the probabilities of two independent events to arrive at the probability of their simultaneous occurrence. Hence, the correct answer is 1:6 × 1:6, or 1:36.

One way to see why adding the probabilities of independent events together is wrong is to ask the same question about the chances of six sixes in a roll of six dice. If we add, then the answer becomes 1:6 × 6, or a probability of one. But there is always a possibility that a toss of six dice will yield an outcome without six sixes. Hence, the likelihood of rolling a pair of sixes is less than some imagine.

Birthday Parties: Also Less Than You Think

Suppose you decide to host a party in which the theme is "Let's Celebrate Our Birthday Together." Your clever idea is to give prizes to those born on the same day and month. How many people do you need to invite to be 99 percent sure that at least two people share the same birthday and therefore go home with thoughtful gifts?

Given that the chances of a person being born on a particular day are 1:365, some mistakenly believe the answer is 0.99 × 365, or 361 individuals. That is the equivalent of adding up the probabilities of 365 independent events. To see why this reasoning is wrong, suppose you invite 365 people. That does not guarantee that two guests will share the same birthday.

In fact, the answer is fifty-seven partygoers.[26]

To arrive at this answer, we could try to multiply together all the possible permutations in which at least two people have the same birthday. But there is a much simpler method: calculate the chances that there is *not* a common birthday between two or more of the guests.

Let's illustrate how to do so with a calendar. Start with the first guest to arrive. Ask them to circle their birthday on a calendar. The probability is 100 percent that the first guest will not draw on top of another circle because the calendar is blank. The odds of the second guest drawing a circle on the date marked by the first guest are 364:365, the third guest 363:365, and so on.

Per Cardano's power rule, we can multiply these independent events together to determine the odds that our guests do not have a common birthday.[27] For example, the chances that our first three guests were born on different days is the product of the odds of each guest circling an unmarked date. For guests one, two, and three, those probabilities are 1, 364:365, and 363:365, respectively. Hence, the likelihood our first three guests have different birthdays is $1 \times (364/365) \times (363/365)$, or 99 percent. Or stated differently, the probability they share a common birthday is 1 percent.

With the arrival of each new guest, we keep calculating the odds of two people not sharing the same birthday by eliminating one day from the numerator and then multiplying the resulting fraction. If you do the math, there is a more than 99 percent chance by guest number fifty-seven that someone will have drawn a circle on top of another. By inviting fifty-seven people, you can be 99 percent certain that at least two of your guests will take home prizes.

A similar example of how we can be misled by probability comes from parties thrown during the 1960s.

Swingers Parties:
A Lot Less Than You Want to Imagine

During the 1960s sexual revolution, people held "swingers parties" in which married couples would randomly pair off for sex with someone other than their spouse at the end of the evening. It was reported that husbands would throw their car keys in a large bowl, and wives, without looking, would withdraw a key from the bowl to determine their partner for the night. Of course, there was some chance that a wife would draw her husband's keys out of the bowl.

Many believed that the larger the swingers party, the greater the number of couples who would end up going home with the person with whom they came, defeating the party's purpose. In other words, a party with fifty couples was thought to have a greater number of wives grabbing the keys of their husbands than a party attended by five couples.

In fact, the number of couples who could expect to spend the night with their spouse is the same for a swingers party of five or fifty pairs of husbands and wives.

Imagine a swingers party with two couples. Two sets of car keys are in the bowl, and so the odds of selecting the keys of your spouse are 1:2. In a swingers party of three couples, the odds are 1:3, four couples 1:4, and so on. Regardless of the number of couples who attend a swingers party, whether five, fifty, or five hundred, we should expect on average only one married couple to end up with a less eventful evening.

We can also calculate the likelihood of going home with your spouse. Your odds are 1:10 for a party with ten couples, and that ratio decreases linearly with each new couple. For example, by increasing the size of the party from ten to one hundred couples, the odds of pairing off with your spouse fall from 1:10 to 1:100, a tenfold decline. This probably led to some interesting discussions among husbands and wives about whether to attend a smaller or larger party.

In addition to the multiplication rule, Cardano also postulated what would later be known as the "law of large numbers." This foundational theory of probability states that the more trials that are performed, the closer the average of those trials will be to the expected outcome. Cardano called this convergence over time "the expectation of a probability variable," a revolutionary concept in the sixteenth century.

At the time Cardano wrote this, gamblers commonly believed that throws of the dice yielded a variety of outcomes, and the average of those outcomes was independent of the number of throws. Cardano did not express his idea of the law of large numbers mathematically, quantify his conclusions, or offer a formal proof. (That would be left to Jacob Bernoulli in 1713, and that is why the law of large numbers is known today as Bernoulli's theorem.) Nevertheless, Cardano was the first to postulate that repeated trials would tend to push the average of the repeated trials toward an expected value. Cardano himself believed that his theory of the law of large numbers was his greatest mathematical achievement.[28]

Given Cardano's addiction to games of chance, he understood the importance of the law of large numbers since it is the basis for the gambler's fallacy.

Striking Out in Monte Carlo

The gambler's fallacy is believing in "hot streaks." The law of large numbers explains why we should not place too much faith in just a few data points, such as a few lucky throws of the dice or turns of the cards.

Let's say we flip a fair coin twice, and it comes up heads both times. That is not a reason to conclude that heads is more likely than tails on the third throw. By Cardano's power rule, there is a 25 percent chance ($1/2 \times 1/2$) of two independent events with equal probability occurring back to back.

One of the most famous examples of the gambler's fallacy occurred on the night of August 18, 1913, at the Casino de Monte-Carlo in the Principality of Monaco.[29] At one of the tables on that hot summer evening, a roulette wheel began a run of landing on black. As word spread throughout the casino, more and more gamblers crowded round the table, wagering increasingly larger amounts of money. Soon, there was a frenzy of betting, as aristocrats and wealthy individuals shoved higher and higher stacks of chips on the table, doubling and tripling their bets. It was reported that gamblers and house managers "watched in awe and distress."[30] For twenty-six consecutive spins, the ball landed on black.

Then it hit red. Fortunes were lost, and several individuals were bankrupted.[31]

The odds of a fair European roulette wheel hitting black twenty-six times in a row are 1:137 million, or less than the chances of an asteroid wiping out the earth. Some believe the roulette wheel that landed on the same color twenty-six times in a row on that summer night in 1913 had an inherent bias. In 1873, an English engineer, Joseph Jaggers, determined after a month of observations that some numbers were more likely to come up than others on a roulette wheel at the same casino. He subsequently won millions of dollars (in today's dollars) until management caught on and switched out the warped wooden wheel. Twenty years later, another Englishman, Charles Wells, did the same and inspired the song, "The Man Who Broke the Bank at Monte Carlo."

I can imagine how a production defect could cause a wooden roulette wheel to favor particular sections, and thus a specific set of numbers. Jaggers and Wells proved this was possible, at least by the manufacturing standards of the nineteenth century.

But I do not see how imperfections could lead to a wheel being significantly biased toward slotting the ball into black. The manufacturing defects would somehow have to match the alternating colors of black and red circling the wheel. Furthermore, you would think that by 1913, after two Englishmen broke the bank, the management of the Casino de Monte-Carlo would have learned their lesson about the importance of quality control of roulette wheels.

In my view, those who bet ever larger amounts of money on black on that balmy night on the French Riviera fell victim to the gambler's fallacy, the belief that "hot streaks" involving random, independent events are more likely than not to continue.

A more recent example of how hot streaks can confuse us comes from modern-day Major League Baseball.[32]

Striking Out in Major League Baseball

One job of a baseball umpire is to call balls or strikes. Major League Baseball (MLB) Rule 2.00 states that the strike zone is established by the stance taken by a batter who is prepared to take a swing.

It is defined as follows:

> *That area over home plate the upper limit of which is a horizontal line at the midpoint between the top of the shoulders and the top of the uniform pants, and the lower level is a line at the hollow beneath the kneecap.*[33]

PITCHf/x is an MLB system that tracks the trajectory and location of the ball as it crosses the plate. Researchers compiled data from 1.5 million pitches called by 127 different umpires over the 2008 to 2012 seasons and looked at pitches that could have been called either way.[34] In the case of these pitches, researchers found that umpires are less likely to call a strike if the previous pitch was also called a strike. And the likelihood of calling a strike is even lower if the two previous pitches that were close calls were also called strikes.

Some have argued that umpires may wish to be fair and undertake "makeup" calls in which they try to correct for a previous incorrect call. In fact, the researchers found the opposite. The less obvious it was that the previous call was a ball, the less likely it was that the next call would be a strike. In addition, the desire to appear to be unbiased would suggest that an error on the last-called pitch for the previous team at bat would be followed by an error in the same direction on the first-called pitch for the opposing team at bat. But no such evidence was found.

In the case of MLB, the impact of recent random events is the opposite of the gambler's fallacy. In Monte Carlo in 1913, many thought black to be more likely to follow black. In modern-day MLB, called pitches are more likely to alternate between balls and strikes.

In my opinion, most feel that the order of called balls and strikes is basically random, and therefore streaks of strikes (or balls) suggest an umpire is biased against a particular player or team. If players, fans, and the management of MLB harbor such suspicions, then umpires may be responding to this belief by unconsciously (or consciously) alternating between balls and strikes. This behavior could be a form of job security or a way to cut down on boos from the fans. In this case, we can just as easily be misled by a forced pattern as by hot streaks.

All the preceding examples were related to puzzles and games of one sort or another. The consequences of being confused by chance were taking home a goat, mistakenly guessing the gender of the child of a stranger, a more or less enjoyable birthday (or swingers) party, and striking out at bat. But real harm can come from being misled by probability.

Two famous court cases are good examples.

Sally Clark: A Jury Misled by Probability

Sally Clark, a British lawyer, gave birth to her first child, Christopher, on September 22, 1996. Less than three months later, on the night of December 13, she found Christopher dead in his crib. Clark gave birth to a second son, Harry, on November 29, 1997, and he died suddenly on January 26, 1998. Sally and her husband were arrested, but the charges against her husband were dropped, as Sally was alone in the house when both children died. In November 1999, Sally was convicted of the murder of her two children and sentenced to life imprisonment.

The defense argued that the infants died from sudden infant death syndrome (SIDS). There is no test for SIDS. A diagnosis is given if no cause of death can be identified in the case of a sudden loss of life by an otherwise healthy infant.

The prosecution claimed that the loss of two babies to SIDS was almost a mathematical impossibility. Sir Roy Meadow, a professor and prominent pediatrician, testified at Clark's trial that the incidence of SIDS death was 1:8,500 per family with infants. He concluded that the odds of a family suffering two SIDS deaths were 1:72,000,000, or 1/8,500 squared. Meadow told the jury that the probability of experiencing two SIDS deaths within the same family was comparable to backing a 1:80 bet at the racetrack and winning four times in a row. Meadow stated that based on his research, "One sudden infant death is a tragedy, two is suspicious and three is murder, until proved otherwise."[35]

After her conviction, Clark was widely condemned in the press around the world as a baby killer. Her husband had to quit his job and sell their house to pay for legal bills. Her appeal from prison in 2000 was denied.

But the jury that convicted Sally Clark was misled by probability. The number of SIDS deaths per family was irrelevant. The jury should have considered the incidence of SIDS deaths compared to infanticide. Murders of infants by their mothers in the United Kingdom average thirty per year.[36] By contrast, the number of SIDS deaths in the United Kingdom is approximately two hundred annually.[37] Thus, the odds that an unnatural and unexplained death of a child is from SIDS rather than murder is 87 percent, or 200:230. In fact, the actual odds are higher. SIDS deaths are positively correlated within families, due to a suspected genetic component. On the other hand, double murders are negatively correlated within families, because after the first murder the homicidal parent, if arrested or convicted, is less likely to be around. These two factors mean the chances that SIDS was the cause of death for Sally Clark's children, based solely on probability, was higher than 87 percent.

Sally Clark's second appeal in 2003 was successful but not for these reasons. In the first trial, the prosecution's pathologist withheld evidence that indicated that Clark's second child, Harry, likely died from an infection. Sally was released from prison but was never the same. She suffered from severe psychiatric problems, deep depression, and alcohol dependency. She was found dead from alcohol poisoning in her home on March 16, 2007. She was forty-two years old.

Before the trial of Sally Clark, Meadow had become famous for his 1997 book, *ABC of Child Abuse*, and had been knighted in 1998. As one juror in another trial in which Meadow testified recounted, "When a scientist is a professor and a Sir, that authority is augmented many times."[38] Before the reversal of Clark's conviction in 2003, Meadow had given testimony in more than one hundred cases concerning the unexplained death of infants. Some resulted in the convictions of mothers for murdering their children.[39]

Of course, the fact that Meadow gave testimony doesn't prove that in each of these cases SIDS was the real cause of death. Perhaps there was other compelling evidence. But Meadow likely played an important part in sending some number of innocent mothers to jail. We do not know how many of these mothers are still behind bars, imprisoned for crimes they did not commit, because a jury was misled by probability.

Confused by the odds, juries have not only convicted the innocent but also acquitted the guilty. An example of the latter occurred in 1995 in a Los Angeles County courthouse.

O.J. Simpson: If the Statistics Don't Fit

On the night of June 12, 1994, Nicole Brown and her friend Ronald Goldman were stabbed to death in Brentwood, a suburb of Los Angeles. Nicole Brown's ex-husband, O.J. Simpson, a retired football player and sometime actor, was arrested and charged with the murders five days later. The police found Brown's and Goldman's blood in Simpson's Ford Bronco and on his socks. Both victims' blood and hair were detected on one of Simpson's gloves. On October 3, 1995, Simpson was acquitted after eleven months in the highly publicized "Trial of the Century."

During seven years of marriage, Simpson abused Brown more than fifty times, although only a handful of those incidents were reported to the police, and Simpson was arrested just once.[40] But Alan Dershowitz, one of the lead defense attorneys, cast the argument for Simpson's innocence in stark statistical terms, telling the jury that each year only 1 in 2,500 abusive husbands murder their wives.[41]

Dershowitz, consciously or not, was misleading the members of the jury. In terms of the statistic cited by Dershowitz, the question is not the probability that an abuser will murder his wife. Few abusers kill their spouses. Rather, the jury should have considered the odds that a murdered battered wife was killed by her husband. When an abused wife is murdered, the husband is usually the prime suspect.

In 1992, 4,936 women were murdered in the United States; 1,432 of those murdered women were killed by their husbands.[42]

Approximately 3.5 million women are battered each year.[43] Hence, the chances that a murdered woman was killed by her husband are 29 percent (1,432:4,936). But given that not all women murdered by their husbands were battered, the probability that a battered woman was murdered by her husband is less than 0.04 percent (1,432:3,500,000).

Since approximately 3.5 million women are battered each year, Dershowitz's claim that only one in 2,500 battered women are murdered by their husbands is approximately right (3,500,000/1,432 = 2,444). However, Dershowitz (and for unknown reasons, the prosecution) failed to mention that it is also true that the odds that a murdered woman has been killed by her batterer are at least 725 times greater (29%/0.04%) than the odds that a battered woman has been murdered by her husband.

Conclusions

Cardano was the first to construct sample spaces, propose the multiplication rule for independent events, and discover the law of large numbers. Whether applied to the Monty Hall question or party problems, the theories he developed enable us to make better decisions based on probabilities. Knowledge of his theories is important because there are real-world consequences when we are misled by probability, such as in the cases of Sally Clark and O.J. Simpson.

Because Cardano's book on probability was written as a how-to guide for gambling, subsequent generations of mathematicians largely ignored his work. Some two centuries later, one of the greatest mathematicians of all time independently discovered several of Cardano's theories, which were then embraced by schools and universities.

The German mathematician who rediscovered some of Cardano's theories is most famous for creating the normal or "bell-shaped" distribution. But he failed to appreciate that in the real world, many things are anything but normal.

CHAPTER 2

Normal Distributions: The Tails Wag the Dog

Johann Carl Friedrich Gauss: Abnormally Smart

Johann Carl Friedrich Gauss (1777–1855) was a German mathematician and physicist who has been called one of the most important mathematicians in history.[1]

Gauss was born in what is now part of Lower Saxony to a bricklayer and his illiterate wife. It was obvious at a young age that Gauss was a prodigy. At three years old, Gauss correctly pointed out a miscalculation in his father's wages. In elementary school, Gauss's math teacher, whip in hand, would walk among the students, punishing those who failed to correctly tabulate their sums. One day, the teacher assigned the class the task of adding up the numbers from 1 to 100. Gauss immediately said 5,050. Incredulous, the teacher walked over to the desk where Gauss sat and demanded an explanation.

The young Gauss provided the following answer:

*100 + 1 = 101, 99 + 2 = 101, 98 + 3 = 101, etc., and
so we have as many pairs as there are in 100. Thus,
the answer is 50 × 101, or 5,050.*[2]

The Duke of Brunswick became aware of the brilliance of the poor boy from Lower Saxony and became his sponsor, enabling Gauss to attend university from the age of fourteen. As a teenager, Gauss made several breakthroughs in algebra and geometry. At twenty-one, he completed *Disquisitiones Arithmeticae*, a textbook written in Latin that is the foundational work of modern number theory. His work on Gaussian logarithms, series, sums, integrals, and integers remains part of mathematics today.

In 1833, Gauss and a coworker invented the telegram and sent the first words known to be transmitted electronically, several years before the American inventor Samuel Morse made his first transmission.[3] But Gauss did not believe in patents and offered his invention to all, royalty free. Gauss was also the first to calculate the mathematical properties of mirrors and discovered what is today called Gaussian optics. As part of this, Gauss devised a system to send messages by bouncing light off of specially shaped mirrors, a precursor to modern fiber optic telecommunications.[4]

Gauss was obsessed with numbers. He kept tabulations in notebooks of the number of paces taken during his daily walks, the monthly incomes of hundreds of German companies, and actuarial tables of adult and infant mortality. Gauss earned a modest living as a professor, but he was also a shrewd investor and accumulated Austrian, Swedish, Prussian, Belgian, and Russian stocks and bonds. By the time of his death, Gauss was the equivalent of a multimillionaire today, all on a teacher's salary.

Gauss also had a tremendous talent for languages. He was

fluent in all the modern European languages and English. He enjoyed American novels, particularly *Uncle Tom's Cabin*, and was fervently antislavery. He was also well read in the ancient languages and published his major works in Latin. At the age of sixty-two, Gauss decided to learn Russian and became fluent within two years. At the time of his death, Gauss had seventy-five volumes of Russian literature in his library, and a visiting Russian minister of state once declared that Gauss's pronunciation was perfect.[5]

But Gauss's personal life was marked by tragedy. His first wife died during the childbirth of their youngest son, Louis. Gauss wrote to a friend, "Last night at eight o'clock I closed the angel eyes in which for five years I found heaven."[6] Five months later, Louis died.

Gauss married again, but his second wife contracted tuberculosis. During her illness, their oldest son, Eugene, incurred substantial gambling debts, which Gauss was forced to pay. After a violent argument with his father, Eugene fled to America. Gauss's second wife died soon thereafter, and Gauss never completely forgave his son, believing Eugene's abandonment of his mother hastened her death. In a letter, Gauss called Eugene "a good-for-nothing American who dishonors my name."[7] In 1837, Gauss's son Wilhelm also immigrated to America to escape business debts he could not repay. Wilhelm became a farmer and used enslaved people on his plantation. For the elder Gauss, this was a tremendous personal embarrassment. Gauss never saw his grandchildren in America. He also had two daughters who lived in Europe, but both were childless and died of tuberculosis.

In 1855, a heart attack felled Gauss at seventy-seven years of age. The local university decided to inspect his brain as part of the autopsy. The doctor in charge reported that Gauss's cerebral cortex had the deepest convolutions he had ever seen.[9]

The Normal Distribution: Convenient

Gauss invented the most commonly used probability distribution, known as the Gaussian or normal distribution. It is also popularly referred to as the "bell-shaped curve" because of its symmetrical, humped shape. Gauss was prompted to create the normal distribution by the discovery of the planetoid Ceres.

In January 1801, Ceres was discovered between the orbit of Mars and Jupiter before disappearing behind the sun.[10] A committee of twenty-four of Europe's most prominent scientists was formed to calculate the orbit of the newly discovered planetoid, or today what we would call a dwarf planet.

They all got it wrong.

At the turn of the nineteenth century, astronomy was an inexact science due to observational errors arising from the poor quality of telescopes. Gauss made three assumptions about the differences between the true and observed location of Ceres to compensate for these measurement errors:

1. There are more small than large errors.

2. The distribution of errors is symmetrical.

3. The arithmetic mean is the most likely true value, regardless of the number and magnitude of the errors.

Gauss spent more than one hundred hours calculating estimates of the errors in the known observations of the planetoid. He input those errors into his newly invented normal distribution and successfully predicted the angle of Ceres to Earth to within half a degree when it emerged from the blinding light of the sun. No other scientist even came close. Gauss was instantly a European scientific celebrity at age twenty-four and would remain so for the rest of his life.

A normal distribution can be defined by just two parameters: a mean and a standard deviation. The mean is the average value, and the standard deviation is a measure of the distance from that average value. In a normal distribution, 68 percent of the population is within one standard deviation of the mean. At two and three standard deviations, the numbers are 95 percent and 99 percent, respectively. The normal distribution is also symmetrical: 34 percent of the population is between one standard deviation above the mean and the mean. Similarly, 34 percent of the population lies between one standard deviation below the mean and the mean.

This is quite convenient.

Let's say we want to calculate the odds that a US adult male is taller than five feet eleven inches. We could construct a table of the heights of all men in the United States, count all the men taller than five feet eleven inches, and then divide by the total number of men in the country. More than one hundred million adult males live in the United States, so this would require a lot of measuring and counting.

On the other hand, the average height for men in the United States is five feet eight inches with a standard deviation of three inches.[11] If the heights of US men are normally distributed, we can immediately conclude there is a 17 percent chance a random US adult male is taller than five feet eleven inches. That is because 34 percent of men are between the mean height of five feet eight inches and one standard deviation away of five feet eleven inches. So, the men who are over five feet eleven inches constitute the remaining 17 percent of the taller half of the male population.

The reader may object that no time and effort are actually saved by this method since calculating the mean of five feet eight inches and the standard deviation of three inches requires constructing a table of the heights of all US men in the first place. With such a table, we would know exactly how tall each US male stands, and so there is no need to rely on the convenient properties of a normal distribution.

But measuring every US male would be expensive and

time-consuming. As a practical matter, the best we can do is measure a portion of the male population. Fortunately, we can use the law of large numbers (see Chapter 1) to assure ourselves that if we randomly measure a significant number of US men, our sample will be representative of the heights of US adult males. But we still will not know the true distribution of the heights of the US male population, either before or after we take our sample. Even if our sample mean is a good estimate, the distribution of male heights could be significantly skewed. Male height may not be symmetrically distributed. Perhaps a lot of men are below average height and only a few are above average.

But others later discovered a way around this problem. They called the solution the central limit theorem.

The Central Limit Theorem: Really Convenient

The central limit theorem states that the sample mean of independent variables, such as the height of US men, will be normally distributed, even if the underlying variables themselves are not. In other words, we do not need to care whether the actual heights of US men are normally distributed because the distribution of the sample means will be.

This is *really* convenient.

Now we do not have to measure every man in the United States to calculate the odds that a man selected at random is taller than five feet eleven. Let's say we take the measurements of one thousand men and rely on the law of large numbers to comfort us that our sample mean is representative. With our sample mean in hand, we can estimate the odds of any given height for a US male. The abnormal is the new normal.

With some variation, this method is commonly used throughout the social and biological sciences. It allows us to estimate probabilities from relatively small sample sets (small when compared to the underlying population). Particularly in fields involving large populations, this is often the only feasible method to estimate probabilities. As a result, it has become the standard method used to calculate probabilities.

And it is frequently wrong.

Fat Tails: Really Inconvenient

In the case of the heights of US males, we have a pretty good idea of the extremes of the distribution, or what are called the "tails." In a normal distribution, the tails are very thin. Recall that in a normal distribution, 99 percent of the underlying population is assumed to be within three standard deviations of the mean. So, if we are confident that there is nothing significant out there in the tails beyond three standard deviations, then we can be equally confident about the probabilities deduced from a combination of the law of large numbers and the central limit theorem.

For example, the world has more than seven billion people, and fewer than ten thousand are estimated to be over seven feet tall.[12] Only sixteen individuals are known to have reached a height of eight feet.[13] The tallest human on record, Robert Wadlow, grew to eight feet eleven inches due to a hypertrophy of his pituitary gland. Sadly, he died at the age of twenty-two in 1940.[14] In any case, we can be confident that no US males living today are more than ten feet tall—or we would have heard about them. On the other side of the height distribution, fewer than 1 percent of US males are under five feet tall.[15] So we can be confident that no ten-foot-tall or one-foot-tall men are creating "fat tails" in the distribution of the heights of US males.

By contrast, consider the distribution of wealth in the United States.

In 2021, the estimated net worth of Jeff Bezos, the wealthiest American, exceeded two hundred billion dollars.[16] In the same year, the median net worth for an American family was $121,760.[17] Using the same methods for determining US male height, we are likely to be misled about the amount and distribution of wealth in the United States.

Assume we take a sample of one thousand random households and compute their net worth. We can be virtually certain that Jeff Bezos will not be part of that sample. Based on our sample of one thousand households, we conclude that the average American family is worth around $120,000, give or take. We then multiply that average wealth by the total number of American households to come up with the total wealth of US families.

The problem is we would be wrong about the total wealth of US families. Jeff Bezos, Bill Gates, and Warren Buffett combined have the same amount of wealth as the entire bottom half of the US population.[18] (To their credit, all three have advocated for higher taxes on the rich, and Gates and Buffett have set forth plans to give away almost all their money.) But, based on our sample, we would conclude that wealth inequality is not a real issue in the United States. The one thousand households in our sample most likely would be clustered around the sample mean we use to gauge net worth.

It is true that our sample mean will eventually converge to a normal distribution. But for fat-tailed distributions, it may take so long that we end up having to sample almost the entire population to get there. We are highly unlikely to come across Bezos, Gates, or Buffett in the first million American households we sample, which defeats the original purpose of sampling. In the presence of fat tails, we can easily be misled by probability.

Among the first to point this out was a brilliant mathematician who wrote in the 1960s about what he called the "wild instability" in many normal distributions. But he was ignored until a former Wall Street trader wrote a book in 2007 about the color of a well-known bird.

Benoit Mandelbrot: Jumping Around

Benoit Mandelbrot was a French-American mathematician who is best known for his work in geometry. He spent more than three decades as a research scientist at IBM with periodic breaks to teach at Harvard University. He was an early pioneer of using computers for research, and he discovered fractals. He also developed the Mandelbrot set, a geometric form that, no matter how closely you look at it, never gets simpler. He left IBM in 1987 for Yale University after the tech company disbanded its pure research division. In 1999, at seventy-five years of age, he became the oldest professor in Yale's history to be granted tenure.[19] He died in 2010 from pancreatic cancer.

In 1962, Mandelbrot wrote an internal IBM research paper about the historical prices of cotton titled, "The Variation of Certain Speculative Prices," which was published the following year in the University of Chicago's *Journal of Business*.[20] As the basis for this paper, Mandelbrot later wrote:

> *I analyzed more than a century of data on US cotton prices and studied the way they had varied daily, monthly, and yearly. The results were clear and irrefutable. Far from being well-behaved and normal as the standard theory predicted, cotton prices jumped widely around.*[21]

Specifically, Mandelbrot discovered that "the empirical distributions of price changes are usually too peaked to be samples from Gaussian populations . . . the tails of the distributions of price changes are in fact extraordinarily long."[22]

This went against the standard model employed by virtually all economists and social scientists at that time; they relied on normal distributions, combined with the law of large numbers and the central limit theorem, as the basis for their research. Mandelbrot noted that his findings had caused quite a stir:

> Like most trade unions, economics departments like to keep a closed shop. So, my cotton research caused a hullabaloo . . . I was about as welcome in the established church of economics as a heretical Arian at the Council of Nicene.[23]

Because he challenged the unquestioned use of normal distributions, the basis for most academic research, Mandelbrot was largely ignored for the next five decades.

That changed during the 2008–2009 financial crisis with the publication of a book by a former Wall Street trader.

Nassim Taleb: Not Fooled by White Swans

Nassim Taleb is a mathematician, former options trader, and the author of several best-selling books, including *The Black Swan*. Born in Lebanon, Taleb grew up in a prominent and politically active family, which included several prime ministers. Taleb came to the United States in 1981 for an MBA and moved to France to attend the University of Paris for his PhD, which was awarded in 1998. Taleb retired from trading during the 2000s to focus full time on writing and lecturing. (Full disclosure: Taleb and I worked together on Wall Street years ago.)

In 2001, Taleb published *Fooled by Randomness*, in which he talks about black swans as an example of the problem of induction. Taleb writes that we "cannot logically make the statement . . . no swan is black because I looked at 4,000 swans and found none."[24] However, we can say that "not all swans are white . . . by merely finding a single black swan."[25]

In 2007, Taleb put out an expanded version of *Fooled by*

Randomness, titled *The Black Swan*, in which he fleshed out three criteria for a black swan event:

1. It is an outlier.

2. It had an extreme impact.

3. Only in hindsight was it foreseeable by most people.

Taleb is often asked what the next black swan event will be, which shows that the questioner has not read Taleb's books. A corollary of the third criterion is that a black swan event is not a well-known risk before it happens. Two planes piloted by terrorists flying into the World Trade Center was a black swan event. But Hurricane Katrina was not a black swan event because storms have washed over New Orleans in the past. In the words of Donald Rumsfeld, the former US secretary of defense, a black swan event is an example of an "unknown unknown."

Taleb agrees with Mandelbrot that the past and the future are not well described by a normal distribution for many things we care about. But Taleb is making the additional argument that we cannot know what that future black swan event will be or when it will occur. Nevertheless, we do know that such an event will eventually occur, and it will be of an extreme magnitude. Even worse, the more unlikely the event, the more extreme it will be when it happens. This applies to things we are familiar with, like earthquakes: the big ones are less frequent but more destructive than the small ones. In *The Black Swan*, Taleb argues that the best we can do is to prepare for severe shocks since black swan events, by definition, are unforeseeable.

Of course, we often try to shield ourselves from knowable risks, even those that are highly unlikely and of an extreme magnitude. Fire and flood insurance are common risk management tools. The problem is that most of us prepare for knowable risks and thus are caught off guard when a black swan event occurs. Taleb uses the example of a casino that reserves sufficient funds to cash out occasional jackpot winners but incurs large uninsured losses to pay a huge ransom for the return of the owner's kidnapped daughter.

The publication of *The Black Swan* was well timed. Less than a year after the book came out, the world was hit by the most severe financial market crisis in eighty years. The New York Stock Exchange has seen many stock market crashes, such as those in 1929 and 1987, after the Arab oil embargoes of the 1970s, and during the bursting of the technology bubble in the early 2000s. But each time, the cause of the dramatic decline in equity values differed.[26] The dramatic drawdown in the market from the summer of 2007 to the spring of 2009 was another black swan event brought on by a blow to the financial system from an unexpected direction.

Not Once in Three Trillion Years

The financial crisis of 2008–2009 was sparked by a collapse of the market for securitized subprime mortgages, financial instruments that had not existed on a large scale until that time. A few people did foresee the dramatic fall in value of this particular strip of mortgage-backed securities. But most investors were confident that the sources of recent equity market collapses (commodity prices, portfolio insurance, foreign debt, rampant speculation in tech stocks) were well in hand and no longer posed a significant threat.

As the crisis unfolded, Wall Street executives rushed to justify their financial risk models. During a conference call with shareholders, the chief financial officer of a major investment bank explained that the firm's losses were due to the markets experiencing "25-standard deviation moves, several days in a row."[27] Assuming stock returns are normally distributed, this would be an unusual series of events. To put this in perspective, a single-day move of seven standard deviations, given a normal distribution, is expected to happen once every three trillion years.[28] The universe is about fourteen billion years old, so twenty-five consecutive standard deviation moves in the stock market must have been quite a surprise. This CFO later said of the experience that it "makes you reassess how big the extreme moves can be."[29]

Perhaps this CFO should reassess his risk models. He should consider being more introspective and learning from the models used every Monday through Friday to make money on the trading floor of his firm.

Volatility Smirks and Clusters

On the derivatives desks of Wall Street firms, including those of the preceding CFO, traders do not assume stock returns are normally distributed.[30] As discussed previously, the assumption of normality is standard practice in economics and the social sciences. The Black-Scholes option pricing model, which is the basis for the risk models used by Wall Street executives, is no exception. (Full disclosure: I worked with the now-deceased Fischer Black at Goldman Sachs and taught a course at the Graduate School of Business at Stanford University with Myron Scholes.)

However, traders are well aware, sometimes from painful, personal experience, that stock returns are not normally distributed. In particular, traders know two things from watching stock prices all day long over the course of many years. One, stock price movements can be extreme, exhibiting fat tails. Two, stock prices jump down more often than up, demonstrating asymmetrical returns around the mean.[31]

So, when pricing options, traders attempt to compensate for the decidedly not normal distribution of stock prices by massaging the volatility assumptions entered into the Black-Scholes option pricing model.

To compensate for fat tails, traders enter higher volatility assumptions into their models compared with historical volatilities as measured by a normal distribution. Hence, stock options typically trade at a higher price than that predicted by historical volatilities based on a normal distribution. In addition, to adjust for the tendency of stocks to jump down more often than up, traders assume a higher level of volatility for out-of-the-money put options than for out-of-the-money call options. (Call options that are the right to purchase a stock at a higher price and put options that are the right to sell at a lower price are considered out of the money.) As a result, out-of-the-money put options are typically more expensive than out-of-the-money call options.[32] This is known as a volatility "smirk," because one side of the volatility curve is lower than the other.

Furthermore, traders know that there is a positive correlation between the direction and magnitude of the price changes. Large price moves tend to be followed by larger than typical price moves, and vice versa.[33] Because volatility "clusters," instability breeds further instability. Yet, the normal distributions underlying Black-Scholes and other financial models presume that future changes in volatility are independent of those in the past. To compensate for the fact that changes in volatility are positively correlated, traders increase (or decrease) the overall implied volatility entered into the Black-Scholes model as a function of the change in the magnitude of recent stock price movements.

The non-normality of stock market prices was well understood on the trading floor—but apparently not in the executive suites. So why didn't the risk models used by senior executives during the 2008–2009 financial crisis mirror those of the traders who work for them?

My view is that the incentives of senior executives on Wall Street differ from those of shareholders and employees. The tenure for most of those running Wall Street firms is measured in years, not decades. (Remember the adage: if you want a friend on Wall Street, get a dog.) Hence, there is an incentive to maximize profits during a CEO's relatively short time at the top. After all, they do not get paid after they leave. Economists call this an "agency" problem. The interests of senior management and shareholders have diverged because the former is trying to maximize profits over a shorter timescale than the latter.

The most common (and easiest) way to increase the profits of a Wall Street firm is to increase leverage. In good times, this works really well. In bad times, not so much. Since extreme events are rare, senior executives can leverage up their firms to increase profits because it is highly unlikely that a black swan event will occur during their tenure.

In addition, senior executives of the largest firms on Wall Street understand that the taxpayers have granted them (through their elected and appointed government officials) a free "put." The largest Wall Street firms that are still around today would have failed during the 2008–2009 financial crisis without capital injections and guarantees from the federal government.[34] Wall Street firms can leverage up their balance sheets and drive up profits during the good times; when bad times come, in the form of a black swan event, they can look for Uncle Sam to rescue them. Economists call this a "moral hazard" problem.

The rationale for bailing out these major Wall Street firms during the 2008–2009 financial crisis was that they were "too big to fail." Those in government argued that the expense of bailing out the banks would be less than the cost to the economy from a series of bank bankruptcies. More than a decade later, these major Wall Street firms are bigger than ever. The largest firm on Wall Street, JPMorgan, has grown to more than $2.5 trillion in assets, nearly twice its size before the financial crisis.[35] To stabilize the banking system, the US Federal Reserve System and US Department of the Treasury forced several large firms to merge. Wells Fargo is now three times its pre-crisis size due to the acquisition of Wachovia.[36] Bank of America's asset size is up by more than 50 percent after the purchase of Merrill Lynch.[37]

The executives of today's larger firms understand they have more leverage than ever over the government and have learned from past experience that withdrawing from the taxpayer piggy-bank comes without penalties. During the 2008–2009 financial crisis, executives at firms bailed out by US taxpayers experienced no adverse consequences. After the government rescued AIG Inc., the company immediately awarded $165 million in executive bonuses.[38] The CEOs of the firms bailed out by the government—Citibank, JPMorgan, Wells Fargo, Bank of America, Morgan Stanley, Goldman Sachs, and Merrill Lynch—all kept their jobs. Most went on to make tens of millions (and some of them hundreds of millions) of dollars in annual compensation for years afterward.

The financial crisis of 2008–2009 was a black swan event. Wall Street CEOs and CFOs claimed it was a fluke, a 25-standard-deviation event, predicted to occur at most once in the history of the universe.

These Wall Street executives may have been genuinely caught unaware. Perhaps they naively believed in their normal distribution models.

Or maybe not.

Stocks are not the only financial instruments whose prices exhibit fat tails. In fact, cryptocurrencies suffer from even more extreme gyrations.

The most commonly held cryptocurrency goes by the name of bitcoin.

Bitcoin: A Tail without a Dog

Bitcoin began on August 18, 2008, when a person or group of persons uploaded to a message board a paper titled "Bitcoin: A

Peer-to-Peer Electronic Cash System" under the name of Satoshi Nakamoto. On January 3, 2009, Nakamoto released open-source code, known as the "genesis block," which launched the first bitcoin blockchain. On April 26, 2011, Nakamoto posted their last anonymous message, stating that they had "moved on to other projects."[39] Before disappearing, Nakamoto had amassed 1.1 million bitcoins in various electronic wallets.[40] As of January 2022, the value of a bitcoin was $41,000, which means Nakamoto was worth $45 billion in US dollars at that time. Nakamoto has yet to spend a single bitcoin, perhaps for fear that doing so will reveal his, her, or their identity.[41]

Today, the total value of all bitcoins is more than one trillion US dollars, constituting about 60 percent of the value of all cryptocurrencies.[42] By comparison, the value of the world's total money supply is estimated at upward of $40 trillion.[43] Although bitcoin is still a small fraction of the total value of all currencies, it has been prominently featured in daily financial headlines due to its meteoric rise in value from less than $100 in 2013 to a high of $69,000 in November 2021.

Not surprisingly, bitcoin is generally thought to be a riskier investment than stocks. For example, the daily volatility of bitcoin is 4.5 times that of the Standard and Poor's 500 Index (S&P 500 Index).[44] Similarly, the distribution of daily returns on bitcoin has demonstrated fatter tails. One study showed that in a comparison of daily price movements during 2018, the S&P 500 Index and bitcoin prices fell outside the normal distribution six versus twenty-eight times, respectively.[45]

The standard deviation of returns and the incidence of fat tails in bitcoin prices are highly sensitive to the measurement period. Based on daily prices, bitcoin suffers from a significantly greater volatility and a greater incidence of fat tails than the S&P 500 Index.[46] By contrast, measured on a monthly basis, bitcoin is actually less volatile and exhibits thinner tails than stocks.[47] From 2013 to early 2021, bitcoin prices have risen more than four hundred times, compared with a meager 3.3 times for the S&P 500 Index over the same period. Hence, the investment appeal of bitcoin is not surprising: a lower monthly volatility combined with a higher historical return.

But as a medium of exchange, bitcoin leaves a lot to be desired. The extreme daily fluctuations in bitcoin prices, particularly compared with the major currencies, mean that consumers and merchants are reluctant to transact using bitcoins. A medium of exchange that can move 5 percent or 10 percent over the course of a day injects unnecessary uncertainty into commercial transactions.

Unfortunately, the historical volatility of bitcoin has become a vicious circle. Because bitcoin has been volatile, it has not been widely accepted as a medium of exchange and so remains largely an investment vehicle. In contrast, international trade dampens currency fluctuations, as goods and services move across borders in response to movements in exchange rates. Furthermore, national governments have an incentive to intervene in currency markets to counteract violent price changes. As of today, governments feel no obligation to tamp down fluctuations in bitcoin prices.

In my view, bitcoin is likely to remain mainly a store of value, an alternative to stocks, bonds, and commodities. As a new asset class, cryptocurrencies have the advantage of being relatively uncorrelated with the returns of all other investments and thus are a good way to diversify existing portfolios. In addition, the total number of bitcoins is capped at 21 million. Central governments, during times of financial distress, have been debasing national currencies by issuing more coins or notes since the days of the Roman Empire. Most public corporations issue more shares if they believe their stock price is highly inflated. Mining companies typically ramp up production in response to rising commodity prices. But bitcoin as a store of value is largely immune to the laws of economics: no amount of additional demand can bring about a greater supply. As an inflation hedge, bitcoin may hold great appeal.

I am not offering investment advice or suggesting that the price of bitcoins will rise or fall in the years ahead. Several types of catastrophic events (that I will not explain here) would make bitcoins nearly worthless. Millions of dollars of bitcoins have been stolen in the past, and a major hack of the underlying source code in the future would undermine trust in the cryptocurrency as a store of value. Another hard fork like the one that occurred in 2017 could spark a cascade of more hard forks that dilute the value of bitcoins.[48] A cabal of bitcoin miners could gain majority control of the network's hash rate[49] and double-spend[50] coins. Fearing a loss of control of the money supply and an inability to police criminal activities, governments could outlaw bitcoin or at least limit its ease of use through onerous regulations.

Unlike stocks, bonds, or commodities, no asset underlies a bitcoin. Some have argued that the fiat currencies of governments likewise have no intrinsic worth: the US Federal Reserve System long ago stopped holding gold reserves equal to the amount of currency in circulation. Nevertheless, governments have an incentive for their respective national currencies to retain some value. Bitcoin is valuable only because someone else believes the same. In that sense, the rise in the value of bitcoins is like the tulip bulb mania that struck Holland during the 1630s. But at least you could plant tulips.

Despite the issues with bitcoin, it and other decentralized peer-to-peer cryptocurrencies are not going away. Throughout history, governments and other institutions have consistently proven themselves to be untrustworthy stewards of the wealth of their citizens. Banks have periodically lost the monies entrusted to them by depositors. Corporations have been known to mislead shareholders. It is not coincidental that the bitcoin was invented during the financial crisis of 2008–2009. Ultimately, bitcoin may not emerge as the dominant cryptocurrency, as the pace of innovation in this space is equal to or greater than that of past technological revolutions. But the notion of creating a store of value through technology that does not depend on politicians or corporate executives has lasting appeal.

The fat-tailed distribution of bitcoin prices has persisted since the day in January 2009 when Nakamoto created the first bitcoin. Just like other financial assets, bitcoin prices do not adhere to a normal distribution. Given the potential for catastrophic events and the uncertainty surrounding cryptocurrencies, I do not expect that to change anytime soon.

Another example of a fat-tailed distribution is deaths from warfare. Because battle deaths and civilian casualties from wars are not normally distributed, we can be misled into believing that the world has become a more peaceful place.

The Long Peace: It May Not Last for Long

Deaths from warfare took a dramatic drop after World War II. Because there has not been a global war in seventy-five years, the latter half of the twentieth century and first two decades of the twenty-first have been called the "Long Peace."

As one prominent author has written: "After 1945, the world's leaders said, 'Well, let's not do that again,' and began to downplay nationalism in favor of universal human rights, international laws, and transnational organizations. The result . . . has been seventy years of peace and prosperity in Europe and, increasingly, the rest of the world."[51]

Battle deaths have declined since 1945, at least in part because a few nations with nuclear weapons have maintained an uneasy global peace. For seven decades after the end of World War II, the

United States and Soviet Union (now Russia) have protected their allies with a "nuclear umbrella." The threat of the use of nuclear weapons, also known as the doctrine of mutual assured destruction, seems to have worked as promised and stopped the outbreak of global wars.

Consistent with the Long Peace is the sharp fall in US defense spending as a percentage of gross domestic product. US defense spending fell from a high of 35 percent during World War II to 5 percent during the later stages of the Vietnam War and Cold War and has dropped to 3 percent currently.[52] Battle deaths per one hundred thousand on a global basis have declined from more than two hundred during World War II to less than five today.[53] Based on the sample set of the last seventy-five years, it appears that the Long Peace is real.

But that would be an unfounded conclusion.

The Fat-Tailed Distribution of Deaths from Warfare

Thousands of wars have been fought throughout history. However, in the nineteenth and twentieth centuries, just a few of those conflicts accounted for most of the deaths. World Wars I and II together constituted 77 percent of all battle deaths during the period from 1820 to 1950.[54] Conflicts during 6 percent of this span of 130 years represented less than 2 percent of the total number of wars fought but were responsible for more than three-quarters of the violence.[55] In short, the number of wars has declined, but the wars that do occur are much more deadly. The distribution of war deaths during the twentieth and early twenty-first centuries has been distorted by fat tails.

A more sophisticated Monte Carlo analysis (a mathematical technique of simulating multiple scenarios) based on the history of conflicts from 1500 to 2018 estimates that a war killing twenty million or more people will occur on average every seventy-three years.[56] This means that the more than seven decades since the end of World War II should not necessarily be viewed as an exceptionally peaceful period.[57]

Not All Battle Deaths Are the Same

The absolute number of deaths from warfare has increased over the past centuries, partly as a function of a rising global population. To adjust for larger population sizes, deaths are often measured on an annual per capita basis. However, this can be misleading. A declining annual per capita death rate may occur because we are killing each other more slowly. The Korean War killed nine hundred thousand people over three years, but the Iran-Iraq War led to 1.25 million deaths over eight years.[58] On an annual per capita basis, the Korean War was more violent.

In addition to the period over which deaths are measured, another issue is defining the number of deaths from battle. Except for the last one hundred years or so, more soldiers died from disease than injury. In 1898, a six-week campaign in the Spanish-American War resulted in 293 casualties from battle and 3,681 from illnesses.[59] The diseases that historically ravaged armies spread easily because tens of thousands of men huddled together in unsanitary conditions far from home. But disease is not the direct consequence of violence; therefore, subtracting battle deaths due to disease dramatically shrinks the total numbers of deaths from past conflicts.

Furthermore, during the twentieth century, the ratio of soldiers wounded to killed has risen sharply. With advances in medical care, each successive generation of soldiers has been able to survive a greater percentage of what previously would have been fatal wounds. Faster transportation and fully staffed field hospitals enable surgeons to operate soon after a soldier is wounded. Modern-day soldiers also have more protection: metal helmets were introduced during World War I, and in later conflicts, soldiers were equipped with flak jackets. For centuries, the ratio of wounded to killed hovered around 3:1. Today, for the US military, that number is closer to 10:1.[60]

In my view, we should not necessarily be comforted by the Long Peace, nor should we believe that conflicts between states have become less violent. Given the fat-tailed distribution of deaths from warfare and the challenges of comparing these deaths over time, the conclusion that the world has become more peaceful is unfounded.

History suggests a war killing twenty million or more is likely to occur every three-quarters of a century.[61] It has been seventy-seven years since the end of World War II.

Let's hope our time is not about up.

Conclusions

More than two centuries ago, Gauss identified and described the normal distribution, and generations of social scientists afterward have taken advantage of its convenient properties in their research. But Mandelbrot demonstrated that much of what we care about is not normally distributed. From the inequality of wealth to the returns from investing in stocks (or bitcoins), we can be misled by probability if we ignore fat tails.

The Long Peace is an example of such a distribution, in which a few outliers in the tails, such as World Wars I and II, account for most of the deaths. Many have come to believe that the world is now a more peaceful place, and hence we should be less concerned about international conflicts. But we should not be misled by probability just because battle deaths in the last seventy-five years have declined. The tail that lies to the extreme right of the distribution of deaths from warfare could be getting fatter with each passing year. If so, then the probability of an international conflict with devastating consequences is greater than ever.

Next, we analyze the basis for our estimates of the likelihood of future events, such as the odds that we might perish in an international conflict. During the eighteenth century, a Scottish philosopher laid out the principles that we still depend on today to make predictions about everything from nuclear wars to coin tosses.

He illustrated his ideas by asking a simple question: what are the odds the sun will rise tomorrow?

CHAPTER 3

Induction: A Mundane System, but It's All We've Got

David Hume: Skepticism and Sunrises

David Hume (1711–1776) was a Scottish philosopher, historian, and economist.[1] Hume was one of the most influential philosophers in Western history and is best known for his book *A Treatise of Human Nature*, published in 1739 when he was just twenty-eight years old. In his book, Hume wrote that we should "reject every system, however subtle or ingenious, which is not founded on fact and observation."[2] Most consider Hume the greatest of the British empiricists. Charles Darwin regarded Hume as a central influence, and Adam Smith credited Hume as the source of many of his theories.[3] Even Albert Einstein said Hume's empiricism was one of the inspirations for his theory of relativity.[4]

Hume was born in Edinburgh to parents of noble ancestry who had some property and not much income. When Hume was only two years old, his father died, and his mother raised Hume and his brother and sister on her own. Hume began attending the University of Edinburgh at the age of eleven but dropped out after four years and never graduated. He later said, "There is nothing to be learnt from a Professor which is not to be met with in Books."[5]

After university, Hume, who never married, lived in one of his father's ancestral homes in Berwickshire on a small allowance from his family. Although his mother wanted him to become a lawyer, Hume determined as a teenager to become a man of letters with "an insurmountable aversion to everything but the pursuits of Philosophy and general Learning."[6] A natural place to pursue his passions would have been a university, but his writings were widely interpreted as espousing atheism. This foreclosed opportunities for a teaching position for fear he would poison young minds. Even one of Hume's closest friends, his fellow Scot Adam Smith, did not advocate for him because it would have jeopardized Smith's own academic post. In fact, despite being one of the greatest philosophers of his century, Hume was never able to obtain a teaching position at a university, despite numerous attempts.

During the 1770s, Hume openly favored American independence. He wrote, "I am an American in my principles and wish we would let them alone to govern or misgovern themselves as they think proper."[7] He once said that he "longed to see America totally and finally in revolt."[8] He was a good friend of Benjamin Franklin and often dined with him on the American's trips to England. When James Madison penned sections of the *Federalist Papers*, he was heavily influenced by Hume's essays.[9] Due to his stance on American independence, Hume was widely vilified in the British press and once commented that "no man is a prophet in his own country . . . I fancy that I must have recourse to America for justice."[10]

Hume seems to have eventually made peace with his critics in the church, academia, and the press. Near the end of his life, he wrote the following:

> *It is not so easy to put right what has once been set wrong, but time does justice to everybody; at least every book. For a man frequently lives and dies under calumny and obloquy; but a book is in a hundred places at once to defend itself and is not so easily susceptible of misrepresentation.*[11]

Throughout most of his life, Hume was obese. He was particularly fond of claret and cheese and was probably afflicted with intestinal cancer. In 1775, Hume fell severely ill and was told he did not have long to live. In his last year, Hume completed his autobiography—a concise 2,972 words start to finish, perhaps the shortest such work in human history composed by a famous writer. Hume began this work with the sentence, "It is difficult for a man to speak long of himself without vanity; therefore, I shall be short."[12]

He concluded his autobiography with these words: "It is difficult to be more detached from life than I am at present. . . . I cannot say there is no vanity in making this funeral oration of myself, but I hope it is not a misplaced one; and this is a matter of fact which is easily cleared and established."[13]

Adam Smith said of his friend after Hume's death:

> *In him certainly attended with the most severe application, the most extensive learning, the greatest depth of thought, and a capacity in every respect of the most comprehensive. Upon the whole, I have always considered him, both in his lifetime and since his death, as approaching as nearly to*

the idea of a perfectly wise and virtuous man as
perhaps the nature of human frailty will permit.[14]

The Problem of Induction

In Book I, Part III, Section VI of *A Treatise of Human Nature*, Hume discusses the problem of induction. He begins by distinguishing between two types of knowledge: the relations of ideas and matters of fact.

We use deduction to reason about the relations of ideas. Hume gave the following example of deductive reasoning: given that all bachelors are unmarried and Person A is a bachelor, we can deduce that Person A is unmarried. Even if everyone in the universe is married, our conclusion is still valid. The relations between the ideas of bachelor, unmarried, and Person A are independent of matters of fact. A similar argument applies to conclusions drawn in mathematics. The Pythagorean theorem describes the relations of ideas within mathematics that are independent of our experience. An infinite number of right triangles can exist, most of which no human has drawn, seen, or imagined. Even if our universe were lifeless, the Pythagorean theorem would still be true.

By contrast, we employ induction to reason about matters of fact. Hume believed that conclusions about direct sensations, or memories of those sensations, could be trusted. In Hume's view, we can be confident that right now we are reading about Hume's problem of induction. We can also be assured that we had pizza for lunch yesterday. So, conclusions about matters of fact in the present or in the past are justified, subject to the imperfections of human impressions and memory.

But Hume believed we get into trouble when we use induction to predict the future. He uses the example of sunrises. For a sixty-year-old person, the sun has risen for more than twenty-one thousand consecutive mornings. But Hume argues that such a person cannot conclude with certainty that the sun will rise tomorrow because this prediction is based on past experience. Consider the analogy of drawing balls out of an urn containing one black and twenty-one thousand white balls. We may initially draw thousands of white balls in succession and wrongly conclude that all the balls in the urn are white.

Hume would agree that a sixty-year-old person would think it is highly probable that the sun will rise tomorrow. This is particularly true since historical records would indicate a much larger sample set than just the twenty-one thousand sunrises personally experienced to date. By comparison, a child should be less confident. In Hume's view, the probability of the sun rising tomorrow is a matter of degree that depends on one's personal experiences and the experiences of others.

Hume did acknowledge that he believed the sun would almost certainly rise tomorrow. He based this belief on what he called the uniformity principle.

The basic idea of the uniformity principle is that we are justified in using induction—if nothing changes. Assuming the same set of circumstances that exist today are in place tomorrow, we can conclude with a high degree of confidence that there will be a sunrise the next morning. We express our degree of confidence by stating the probability that something will happen next.

Probability estimates are a function of the degree of uniformity between the past and the future, which can vary. Take the example of dropping a pencil. The physical conditions that impact the drop of a pencil are largely constant. If I drop a pencil tomorrow, it is highly likely that it will fall to the floor just like it did today and all the days before. By contrast, consider the case of predicting stock prices. Economic conditions and the perceptions of buyers and sellers are in constant flux day to day. We don't know for certain whether the market will rise or fall tomorrow, regardless of what we have previously experienced.

Physics is more uniform than economics, and thus our probability estimates for the sun rising tomorrow are a lot higher and more certain than probability estimates predicting the level of the S&P 500 Index. Of course, the sun could explode overnight. But the chances of Earth becoming untethered to the sun and spinning off into space tomorrow are a lot less than those of a surprising unemployment number. For the physical sciences, in contrast to the social sciences, the past is more likely to be prologue.

Nevertheless, Hume believed that in matters of fact concerning the future there was no absolute certainty, even concerning sunrises. This was Hume's problem of induction. A consequence of the problem of induction is that we can only make statements about matters of fact related to the future in terms of the odds something might occur. As such, probability is a fundamental part of our lives.

Because Hume contended that human beliefs about the future can only be stated in probabilistic terms, during his lifetime he was labeled a skeptic and an atheist and was ridiculed by many for his critique of human reasoning. Hume's formulation of the problem of induction undermined the foundations of rational thought that philosophers had relied on since the time of the Ancient Greeks. Hume argued that we cannot really be absolutely sure about anything that pertains to the future. Certainty lies only in the past and the present.

In response, many have subsequently proposed solutions to the problem of induction laid out by Hume more than two centuries ago.

The Best Explanation:
Trading One Problem for Another

One proposed solution to the problem of induction is called inference to the best explanation (IBE). The basic idea is that whatever hypothesis provides the "best" explanation must be true. Assume a pair of dice is cast multiple times, and in every instance, it comes up snake eyes, or two ones. Many explanations are possible. Perhaps the person tossing the dice manipulated them telekinetically to make them tumble to an unlikely outcome. Or perhaps very small aliens inside the dice pulled levers to determine which side of the dice landed face up. But most people would conclude the dice were loaded.

The problem is that this outcome could also have been a product of chance. Per the gambler's fallacy, we should not reach firm conclusions based on the idea of a hot streak, or an unexpected outcome from a small number of data points. It might just be random chance, which in this case happened to be a lucky outcome.

Another problem is that the objective criteria for what constitutes the best explanation is unclear. Without objective criteria, the best explanation is in the eye of the beholder and could easily vary among individuals. Assume we could somehow establish objective criteria, such as a preference for explanations with fewer assumptions or for explanations that are more consistent with outcomes in related fields of inquiry. Those objective criteria are presumably based on past experiences. Thus, we are relying on induction to support our faith in induction.

In my view, IBE does not solve the problem of induction posed by Hume. Without objective criteria, IBE trades the problem of induction for the problem of defining "best" and relies on circular logic, invoking induction to justify a belief in induction.

Induction Justifies Itself: Round and Round

Some claim that the use of induction to justify induction is acceptable if induction is not used as part of the process. This line of thinking is known as the inductive justification of induction.

Its proponents employ induction to prove the uniformity principle but not to prove induction itself. The way out of the problem of induction for those who espouse this line of thinking is to let the uniformity principle guide our confidence in our probability estimates. In the case of dropping a pencil, we can be virtually certain that the laws of physics on earth will not change, and the pencil will fall to the floor. In the instance of stock market predictions, we should be less confident about our forecasts.

Nevertheless, we learned in the twentieth century that the physical sciences are anything but regular in the ordinary sense of the word. The laws of physics are cited as an example of one of the regularities in nature, but that reflects a Newtonian view of the world. General and special relativity prove that regularity is observer dependent, and quantum mechanics shows us that at the microscopic level the world is anything but constant or predictable. Even a uniformity principle based on physics is not so uniform.

Moreover, our confidence in the uniformity principle is itself based on induction. We use induction to determine the areas in which there is a higher degree (physics) and lower degree (economics) of uniformity. This takes us back to the problem of circular logic because we are relying on induction to justify a belief in induction.

Many have proposed solutions to Hume's problem of induction (unsuccessfully, in my view), but others have taken a different approach and attacked Hume's framing of the issue.

True Colors: Green and Grue

Nelson Goodman recast Hume's formulation as "the new riddle of induction" in his 1955 paper of the same title.[15] Goodman claimed that "what is commonly thought of as the Problem of Induction has been solved or dissolved."[16] He argued that the new riddle is how to "formulate rules that define the difference between valid and invalid inferences."[17]

To illustrate, Goodman provided the hypothetical example of two types of emeralds: green and grue.[18] Green emeralds are always green. Grue emeralds are green until time t in the future, at which point they turn blue, but we do not know which emeralds will turn blue or when they will change.

We are presented with a green and a grue emerald and asked to pick the green one. We observe both carefully for days. Based on induction and the uniformity principle, we have no reason to believe that the physical properties of emeralds will change since they have never done so in the past. But we cannot make a valid inference about which is the green emerald, despite invoking Hume's uniformity principle.

Goodman summarized the problem as follows:

> *All those [emeralds] examined before time t are green; and this leads us to expect, and confirms the prediction . . . [But] this does not lead us to expect, and does not confirm the prediction, that the next one will be grue . . . To say that valid predictions are those based on past regularities, without being able to say which regularities, is thus quite pointless.*[19]

Goodman said we can only rely on those regularities that are "lawlike."[20] In this case, the lawlike regularity required is that green emeralds stay green. He concludes that induction is a valid form of reasoning once we have identified the appropriate lawlike regularities.

But Goodman did not define a method, outside of induction, to determine which regularities are lawlike. He did assert that given enough time we should be able to identify lawlike regularities with certainty; however, he did not show us a way to determine how long is long enough. In our emerald example, we do not know we need to wait until time t.

In any case, what ultimately defeats Goodman's contention that induction works in instances in which there are lawlike regularities is that this claim itself is based on induction. Other than basing his proposition on past experiences, how can he demonstrate that induction based on lawlike regularities can determine the difference between valid and invalid inferences? Goodman's argument, like the others discussed previously, is ultimately a circular logic, calling on induction to justify induction.

Others have attacked the problem of induction by arguing that, as a practical matter, it is not really a problem.

Karl Popper: Not False but Unverified

Karl Popper was an Austrian-British philosopher who wrote several best-selling works on politics and science. He is best known for his book *The Open Society and Its Enemies*, in which he advocated the virtues of liberal democracy and tolerance.[21] Popper was also one of the most influential philosophers of science in the twentieth century.

In his 1963 book, *Conjectures and Refutations: The Growth of Scientific Knowledge*, Popper wrote, "I approached the problem of induction through Hume. Hume, I felt, was perfectly right in pointing out that induction cannot be logically justified."[22]

Although Popper believed the problem of induction had no solution, he was convinced that scientific progress was possible based on what he called critical rationalism. The fundamental tenet of critical rationalism is that scientific theories cannot be verified but can be falsified.

Take the example of the sun rising in the morning. Popper held that it could never be verified that the sun will rise each morning due to the problem of induction. Nevertheless, the theory that the sun rises each morning could be falsified by one instance of the sun not rising. Thus, scientific progress is made by proposing theories and then subjecting those theories to rigorous testing. Theories that are falsified are discarded. The remaining theories are then accepted until they themselves are falsified and replaced by new unfalsified theories.

In Popper's view, those seeking to solve the problem of induction are like the man looking for his keys under the lamppost because that is the only part of the street that is brightly lit. Popper would agree there is value in looking—but only to prove that the keys are not there. Then the man can move on to search less well-lit parts of the street.

Popper's critical rationalism has at least two problems.

One, it does not tell us which of the theories that have not been falsified we should accept. Consider the case of Darwinism versus creationism. Many people believe that neither Darwin's theory of natural selection nor the theory of Creation in Genesis has been disproven beyond a shadow of any doubt. Most people would agree that the evidence overwhelmingly favors Darwin, but we cannot say that creationism has been definitively falsified.[23] Popper himself seems to have realized this was a problem and wrote that those theories that have not been falsified but are more consistent with our experience should be favored over others. Popper would agree that there is a lot more evidence favoring Darwin, and therefore we should accept the theory of evolution over the idea of a divine spark. But we use induction to determine which theories fit our observations. Hence, Popper's critical rationalism brings us right back to the problem of induction.

Two, it is not clear how the principle of falsification in practice is all that useful. Imagine two competing theories about why the sun rises each morning. One is based on the laws of physics, and the other asserts that aliens use tractor beams to move planets around the sun for their own amusement. Neither theory has been falsified, yet one seems a lot more credible. Popper does not provide a method to decide between two unfalsified theories that are equally consistent with our observations. In addition, a strict adherence to Popper's critical rationalism would result in our abandoning some quite useful theories. An example is Newtonian physics. Einstein showed that when things move very fast, Newtonian physics does not apply. Similarly, Schrödinger and others proved that Newtonian physics breaks down when things are very small. By Popper's criteria, Newtonian physics has been falsified. But the fact that Newton was wrong when things move very fast or are very small does not mean we should discard Newtonian physics. The practical application of Newtonian physics to our daily lives allows us to predict what will happen next when we strike a billiard ball or drive a car.

Popper is not the only philosopher of science who rejected Hume's framing of the problem of induction. The most famous philosopher of science of the twentieth century claimed that the basis of human knowledge was even less secure than Hume or Popper believed.

Thomas Kuhn: Shifting Paradigms

Thomas Kuhn was an American philosopher of science whose 1962 book *The Structure of Scientific Revolutions* pioneered the idea of paradigm shifts in human knowledge.

Kuhn outright rejected Popper's description of the scientific process. In direct opposition to Popper, Kuhn argued that, in fact, scientists mainly seek to verify existing theories. In Kuhn's view, scientists regularly ignore evidence that their theories are wrong until the evidence against their theories is so overwhelming that there is no choice but to abandon the current paradigm. Kuhn thought Popper had it backward.

An example is the discovery of the planet Uranus in 1781 by William Herschel.[24] After the planet's discovery, scientists used

Newton's laws of physics to calculate its expected orbit. They found a problem immediately: the path Uranus took around the sun differed significantly from the one predicted by Newton's laws. Uranus seemed to provide evidence that Newtonian physics was wrong.

But scientists did not reject Newtonian physics as a consequence of this evidence. Instead, they held firm to the existing paradigm of Newton's laws of motion and went looking for other explanations. One of those possible explanations was that there was an as yet undiscovered planet whose gravitational pull was influencing Uranus's path through the sky. To find evidence in support of this explanation, scientists trained their telescopes on the night skies, and in 1846, Johann Galle discovered Neptune.

The tendency to hold on to existing belief systems is similar to an argument that could be imagined between a Darwinist and a creationist.[25] The Darwinist argues that creationism is not a valid paradigm given that some fossils are millions of years old, predating 4004 BC, the date many creationists believe God brought forth the world out of darkness. The creationist response could be that God, in 4004 BC, created fossils that were millions of years old.

Kuhn did not believe that scientists were like the creationists, unwilling to abandon their worldview, even when presented with compelling evidence. Rather, Kuhn was making a historical and sociological observation that most scientists (and most people) are slow to discard an existing paradigm. Scientists are no different from other people and tend to filter new evidence through the lens of existing beliefs. Hence, they are naturally inclined to resist paradigm shifts. They first look for verification and only later seek falsification.

Kuhn compared the structure of scientific revolutions to evolution. A species will be resistant to dramatic change until predators or a disruption in food sources forces it to do so. He went on to say that the progress of science, like evolution, will not necessarily be solely in a forward direction. In reaction to their environment, some species have, arguably, taken a step back in the hierarchy of living organisms. For example, bees are descended from dinosaurs. Similarly, Kuhn thought science will not automatically move forward to ever greater heights of human understanding. As Kuhn once said, Aristotle's physics was "simply different rather than inferior to Newtonian physics."[26] Not surprisingly, Kuhn's views on scientific revolutions were rejected by Popper and many scientists. Kuhn seemed to be claiming that science rested on an unstable foundation because scientists refused to let go of the established paradigm.

In my opinion, Kuhn was simply observing that scientists are people too and subject to the same cognitive errors as the rest of us. Science is not a cure-all remedy for ridding scientists of all defects in human reasoning.

It is just better than no medicine at all.

But despite the efforts of many thinkers over the last three centuries, we still do not have a solution to Hume's problem of induction. We cannot be certain about matters of fact concerning the future. But at least we can be confident in our reasoning about the relations of ideas.

Or maybe not.

Relations of Ideas Redux

While Hume questioned the validity of reasoning about matters of fact concerning the future, he maintained that we can be certain about the relations of ideas. Logical syllogisms, as in the case of the unmarried bachelor, and mathematics, as in the Pythagorean theorem, use deductive reasoning to reach conclusions. Hume maintained that the relations of ideas were not subject to the problem of induction.

But how do we know that deduction works?

Humans have been using deductive reasoning for thousands of years, starting at least as far back as the Ancient Greeks. Millions of logical syllogisms and mathematical equations have yielded noncontradictory answers. Based on past experience, we have concluded that deduction is a valid and powerful method of reasoning.

However, this is no different than drawing white and black balls out of an urn. In this case, let's imagine a virtual urn filled with twenty-one thousand logical syllogisms that are noncontradictory and one that contradicts itself. We are likely to draw out thousands of noncontradictory examples before coming upon the one that yields a contradictory conclusion. We ultimately rely on induction, the takeaways from our past experiences with deduction, to assure ourselves that deductive reasoning always works.

This implies that anything we say about the future, including those conclusions based on deductive reasoning, can only be stated in probabilistic terms. If this is true, then all statements have a degree of uncertainty, including those about the relations of ideas. Deduction seems to work because it has in the past, but that does not mean it will necessarily work in the future.

You may object that I am proposing an impossible standard for human reasoning that condemns us to a world of uncertainty in which probability is a fundamental part of our existence. I seem to be claiming that any statement, even those about the relations of ideas, must be couched in terms of probabilities.

Exactly.

Randomness: Not Truly Random

To illustrate my point, let's take the example of tossing a fair coin. By deductive reasoning, we know that the outcome will be either a head or a tail and that both outcomes have the same probability.

However, if the toss of the coin each time were truly identical, then we would always get the same result. As mentioned in the Introduction, if we knew the exact twitches of muscles in the hand, the air currents in the room, the irregularities on the surface of the table, etc., then we could know with 100 percent certainty the outcome beforehand—the process would not be random.

We could try to construct a machine with a mechanical hand that tossed coins in a vacuum onto a perfectly flat table to create a process with a certain outcome. However, that machine and table would be built by nonrandom humans, and so there will be nonrandom imperfections in both. Alternatively, we could try to program a computer to generate random numbers to determine how the coin was tossed. But those supposedly random numbers would arise from lines of code that are written by nonrandom humans.

Some have claimed that truly random processes can be found at the level of quantum mechanics. But the outcomes of quantum mechanics are the products of an interaction with an observer. Without an observer, there is no process to observe. But no observer is completely random in their observations, given that observers themselves are nonrandom living organisms with persistent biases and imperfections.

In fact, no process can be truly random unless the source that generates that process is random itself. But that prompts the question of how to construct a random source.

We should not be surprised that nonrandom inputs result in nonrandom outputs. Our deductive reasoning that a fair coin toss randomly generates, on average, equal numbers of heads and tails is not deductive reasoning at all. In fact, there is no basis to conclude that a truly random process could, in fact, exist. We hold on to our belief about the expected outcomes from tossing a fair coin based on having witnessed outcomes with approximately the same numbers of heads and tails. Hence, even a simple statement like "tossing a fair coin will generate a random series of heads and tails" is ultimately based on induction.

If we accept that deduction is based on induction and that induction has a degree of uncertainty, then there are only two types of statements we can make that are not probabilistic: matters of fact about sensations in the present and memories about matters of fact in the past. These two types of statements appear to be the only ones we can rely on with certainty.

But maybe not.

We Reason to Survive—
Not the Other Way Around

Humans have been appropriately called the "symbolic species."[27] Our ability to use symbols to share information is unique among all creatures on earth. Our facility with symbols not only enables us to process information but also to store this information outside the limited storage capacity of the brain for retrieval at a later date.

But our brains and the symbols within have been shaped by evolution. Through the process of natural selection, the lump of meat inside our skulls and the abstract symbols and images that course through tightly packed wet neurons have been modified to drive behaviors that produce the most offspring.

Hence, the symbols in our brain have not evolved with the primary objective of portraying an accurate depiction of the world around us. Rather, evolution has shaped our brain and the symbols within in ways that favor more children above all else, even if that means misrepresenting the true nature of objects right in front of us. Therefore, we cannot be sure that immediate sensations and memories, the matters of fact as Hume called them, are an accurate portrayal of the external world.

The prominent cognitive scientist Steven Pinker has written:

We are organisms, not angels, and our minds are organs, not pipelines to truth. Our minds evolved by natural selection to solve problems that were life-and-death matters to our ancestors, not to commune with correctness.[28]

The Thing and the Idea-of-the-Thing

The distinction between the symbols that rattle around in our brains and the actual things they represent is at least as old as the writings of the Ancient Greeks. Plato wrote of flickering images cast onto the walls of a cave by objects illuminated by a fire. In more modern times, this distinction has been taken up by philosophers, such as Immanuel Kant, who distinguished between the "thing-in-itself" and the "idea-of-the-thing."[29] Due to this separation, we cannot assume that images or symbols in our brains accurately represent the world out there.

In fact, they don't. I am looking at my computer screen as I type this, and what I see is not what is really in front of me. In my mind, the idea-of-the-thing is a computer screen displaying a bunch of letters, icons, etc. and not the thing-in-itself, which is almost entirely empty space and some subatomic particles whizzing about (or energy waves, if you are of a quantum mechanical mind). However, it is not useful or necessary for me to drill down any further than the level of my computer to write these sentences. I do not even need to go to the level of the pixels on my screen, or the microprocessor that generates the pixels. My brain is quite efficient and expends the least amount of energy necessary to get the job done. In this case, my brain perceives a keyboard, a mouse, and a screen, which are all I need to type out these words.

Similarly, we do not need to count and categorize the molecules that make up an orange to know it is delicious. The image of an orange is a shortcut that tells us all we need to know. Or consider the sudden appearance of a tiger. We do not need to analyze the billions of particles that make up a tiger, compile them into an array, and recall that this pattern fits a predator. The image of a tiger is all the information we need to know that movement is urgently required lest we become a delicious meal. In this case, a quick answer is better than a precise rendering of billions of tiger cells that may take minutes to compile. The latter would also be unnecessary and a waste of limited brain capacity and energy. The idea-of-the-thing evolved to fit the demands of survival, not to accurately portray the thing-in-itself.

Color is another example of an idea-of-the-thing but does not exist independently as a thing-in-itself. In fact, color is entirely species specific. A human eye can detect only a thin wedge of the electromagnetic spectrum. Our eyes pick up light with wavelengths between four hundred and seven hundred nanometers.[30] The rest of the spectrum—radio waves, microwaves, X-rays, and Wi-Fi—pass by us every day, unnoticed.[31] This slight sliver of visible light hits seven million cones and 120 million rods in the human iris, and then the nerves of the eye squash it down to one million signals to be forwarded to the brain.[32] The brain, in turn, decodes and corrects errors from those signals to construct a mental image.[33] What we think of as "red" is the result of this process. But there is no such thing as "red" in the external world. Color is entirely species specific, and other species have entirely different perceptions of color. For example, dogs are thought to perceive red and brown as the same color. Other species perceive color where *Homo sapiens* perceives nothing at all—many birds and fish pick up ultraviolet light.

The perception of time is also species specific. For a fly, time passes at a pace seven times slower than that of a human.[34] Time moves more slowly for a fly because its eyes send signals to its brain seven times faster than the eyes of *Homo sapiens*. This explains why flies are so hard to swat. Dogs perceive that time moves twice as slowly as humans for the same reason.[35] This partly accounts for dogs' fascination with television—they see the flickers between images. By contrast, for humans, time moves at three times the pace than that perceived by a leatherback turtle.[36] In the underwater world of a turtle, movements of predators happen more slowly than on land, so the ability to react quickly is less important for survival. Even the moment when something happens is species specific. In humans, visual experience arises in the brain 150 to 350 milliseconds after light enters the eyes, but that is different for other animals as well.[37]

Francis Crick, a co-discoverer of RNA and DNA, wrote, "Seeing is an active, constructive process . . . a symbolic interpretation of the world . . . in fact, we have no direct knowledge of the objects in the world."[38]

Einstein expressed a similar view much earlier: "Time and space are modes by which we think, and not conditions in which we live."[39]

The preceding is not to claim, as some philosophers have over the centuries, that the idea-of-the-thing is the only thing that is real. This philosophy, known appropriately as idealism, can be disproven by an experiment involving the human brain. Take your head and bang it against the wall. If unconvinced, repeat. There are real things out there. They can hurt you. They are just not what they seem to be.

We See What Darwin Wants Us To

The difference between what is and what seems to be is determined by a species-specific interface. This interface is composed of senses that input data and a brain that processes the information received. However, this interface is biased: it has been shaped by evolution to yield beliefs and behaviors that produce more babies.

Our species-specific interface can be compared to a translator whose job is to render the foreign language of the thing-in-itself into our native tongue of the idea-of-the-thing. But the translator does not faithfully render the text—it has an agenda and cannot be trusted. And we do not speak the foreign language, so we do not know what is the truth or a clever deception.

Another prominent cognitive scientist, Donald Hoffman, wrote:

> *Space and time themselves are simply the format of our interface, and physical objects are icons that we create on the fly as we attend to different options for collecting fitness payoffs. Objects are not preexisting entities that force themselves upon our senses. They are solutions to the problem of reaping more payoffs.*[40]

Hence, the best we can hope for is to understand the biases of the interface of our species and then try to correct for them. This is easier said than done.[41] Part of the problem is that we use our interface to understand our interface.

The linguist Noam Chomsky has said that "some differently structured intelligence might regard human mysteries as simple problems and wonder that we cannot find answers, much as we can observe the inability of rats to run prime number mazes because of the very design of their cognitive nature."[42] This may explain why we cannot understand how consciousness arises from a mass of nerves bundled together atop a spinal cord. The interface of our species evolved to be able to ask many questions but only answer those that mattered. Problem-solving related to the next meal or a nearby predator was important to survival. Pondering how consciousness arose from three pounds of wet meat, not so much.

Other species have similar constraints. If Darwin tried to explain evolution to his dog, the interface of man's best friend prevents that conversation from being productive. From the point of view of evolution, that is acceptable. Having an informative chat about the zoological implications of data collected on a voyage to the Galápagos Islands does not lead to more puppies. A dog with a profound case of ennui due to the meaningless of the universe would be less eager to sniff hundreds of backsides to find a mate.

We should not be surprised. The ability to answer to anything other than pressing life-and-death questions, until recently in human evolution, was a waste of limited brain size and precious energy. Reading (or writing) books about how to solve the Monty Hall or birthday problem is the product of a symbolic species that is no longer concerned about the hungry lion crouching in the nearby tall grass.[43]

Human perception depends on a species-specific interface that has been designed first and foremost to spread our genes. The same applies to our reasoning. Natural selection is fine with us coming to conclusions that lead to more children. An accurate representation of the world around us was not evolution's primary design criterion.

Hence, we should be skeptical about the conclusions we reach about matters of fact or relations of ideas. Our species-specific interface, the translator between the thing-in-itself and the idea-of-the-thing, has its own agenda. That agenda includes messing with our perceptions of sensations and inductive reasoning to yield more offspring.

Let's assume for the sake of argument that the Darwinian version of the software that natural selection has loaded into our brains does not have any major bugs. We still need to answer the question of why we should trust induction in the first place. But when we ask why we should trust induction, the only answer we can give is, itself, based on induction. This leads to an infinite loop of induction justifying induction.

Conclusions

In *Dialogues Concerning Natural Religion*, Part IV, Hume wrote:

> *If the material world rests upon a similar ideal world, this ideal world must rest upon some other; and so on, without end. It were better, therefore, to never look beyond the present world . . . When you go one step beyond the mundane system, you only excite an inquisitive humour which is impossible to satisfy.*[44]

Hume was referring to the infinite regress of the argument concerning the existence of God. Assume nothing can be created out of nothing and nothing can create itself. If that is true, then something must have created God. But once you tell me Being Alpha created God, then I will ask who created Being Alpha, and so on.

The same applies to induction. Asking the justification for believing in induction is like asking who created God—the answer leads to an infinite regress. Similarly, any answer as to why we should believe in induction relies on the same circular logic. It is induction all the way down.

Hume called induction a "mundane system." He was right. But it is all we've got.

Among those who vehemently disagreed with Hume's writings was a Welshman who was a committed Christian. This philosopher and minister believed he had found a practical solution to the problem of induction in the unpublished papers of a friend who had recently passed away. He believed this discovery was important because it could be used to refute Hume's arguments against the existence of God.

He named the solution after his deceased friend. He called it Bayes' theorem.

CHAPTER 4

Bayes' Theorem: Posterior Is the New Prior

Richard Price: Defender of the Faith and America

Richard Price (1723–1791) was a Welsh philosopher, mathematician, political scientist, and one of the founders of actuarial science.[1] Widely regarded by his contemporaries as one of the leading thinkers of his age, Price is known today for uncovering and developing Bayes' theorem. He was active politically, supporting the French and American revolutions and corresponding regularly with leaders of both movements, including George Washington. He was also a Fellow of the Royal Society and friends with many prominent British religious, political, and literary figures.

Born in Wales, Price was the son of a well-known nonconformist minister from a wealthy family and his second wife.[2] When Price was sixteen, his father died and asked to be buried next to his first wife, leaving Price's mother only a feather bed, bedclothes, and household goods. The bulk of his father's estate went to the children of his first marriage. Less than a year after her husband passed away, Price's mother succumbed to illness. On her deathbed, Price's destitute mother reaffirmed her unquestioning belief in God. She asked and received Price's commitment to dedicate his life to Christianity.

After his mother's death, Price set out for London at the age of seventeen and arrived with not much more than the clothes on his back. He was awarded a scholarship to the Tenter Alley Academy at Moorfields in London. The academy was a strict secondary school run by nonconformists (also known as dissenters) for intellectually inclined young men who, because they refused to pledge allegiance to the tenets of the Church of England, were denied admission to state-sponsored institutions such as the universities of Cambridge or Oxford. While enrolled at the Tenter Alley, Price read and studied widely, including his favorite subject, mathematics. Price was a dedicated student and, unlike many young men of his age, uninterested in city nightlife. At that time, London was renowned for "ribaldry and sexual dissipation" with "printed guides for prostitutes" where "one night with Venus (or a molly-house Apollo) could lead to a lifetime of Mercury."[3] His reaction to the decadent metropolis after leaving the countryside of Wales was a "puritan concentration on industry, sobriety, thrift and prudence."[4]

In 1744, Price graduated from Tenter Alley and secured a position as a nonconformist minister in a local church, then in 1756, he received an inheritance and a townhouse in London from a rich uncle. Price married a year later and moved with his bride to Newington Green, where he resided for the next three decades and continued to serve as a nonconformist minister. He was visited at his home by Thomas Jefferson, John Adams, Thomas Paine, and his lifelong friend, Benjamin Franklin. Other visitors included Adam

Smith and David Hume. Price was also a close friend of Mary Wollstonecraft, a founder of modern feminism, and found a publisher for her controversial books espousing women's right to vote.

During this time, Price published several successful books promoting liberalism and democracy and many best-selling pamphlets, including "A Review of the Principal of Morals." In this pamphlet, Price wrote that we intuitively perceive our "Duty to God" and then to ourselves as "if it is my duty to promote the good of another, and to abstain from hurting him; the same, most certainly, must be my duty with regards to myself."[5] This reasoning foreshadowed *The Critique of Pure Reason* by Immanuel Kant, who refers to Price in his letters some twenty years later.

Price was also one of the founders of actuarial science. In 1768, the Equitable Life Assurance Society hired him to restructure its life insurance business. This led him to publish *Observations on the Reversionary Payments* in 1771, which became a foundational text in actuarial science and one of the first to show how to properly charge for and fund annuities. As a result of this work, insurance societies across Great Britain reset premiums and payouts, and Parliament passed a private pension reform bill. Price was also the first to put forward an actuarially sound proposal for state pensions for elderly people, which was approved by the House of Commons in 1772 but rejected by the House of Lords. He has been called the "Father of Old Age Pensions."[6]

In 1776, Price published a pamphlet that was widely read in England, France, Germany, and North America that expressed support for American independence. He soon became recognized as one of the leading intellectuals and religious ministers in Great Britain in favor of freeing the Colonies. Not surprisingly, his writings on independence were particularly popular in the soon-to-be new nation, although his antislavery stands drew criticism in the American South.

Price was offered US citizenship in 1778 and was invited by the Continental Congress to travel to America as an advisor to the new government, and "if he shall think it expedient to remove with his family to America and afford such Assistance, a generous Provision shall be made for requiting his Services."[7] Although Price was flattered, he turned down the offer, preferring to stay in London and continue writing and preaching. In 1781, Yale University awarded two honorary doctor of law degrees: one to Price and the other to George Washington. Price died at the age of sixty-eight and was buried near his friend Thomas Bayes.

Price and Bayes: Refuting Hume

The books and essays of Hume were well known to Price. To refute Hume's arguments in favor of atheism, some theologians, such as Price, cited "miracles" as proof of the existence of God.

In his 1748 essay "Of Miracles," Hume questioned the reliability of the reports of miraculous occurrences:

> *When anyone tells me, that he saw a dead man restored to life, I immediately consider with myself, whether it be more probable, that this person should either deceive or be deceived, or that in fact, which he relates, should really have happened. I weigh one miracle against the other . . . and always reject the greater miracle.*[8]

In response to Hume, Price wrote in one of his pamphlets, "Let them not pretend they are able to prove a priori, that no accounts of miracles can be true."[9]

Price went on to explain that when we observe a natural event, we often expect it will happen again. Furthermore, the strength of our expectation is proportionate to the frequency with which the event has happened in the past. However, "we have no absolute proof that it will happen in any particular future trial; nor the least reason to believe that it will always happen."[10]

Price had turned Hume's problem of induction back against the Scottish philosopher. Even if miracles had not occurred or were infrequent in the past, we cannot say with certainty that miracles could not happen in the future. Price believed Bayes' theorem was a practical solution to the problem of induction and could refute the arguments of atheists, such as Hume, that it could be "proved" that God did not exist.

Like Price, Bayes was a nonconformist minister and mathematician. Bayes had attended Tenter Alley Academy some twenty years before Price, and the two men shared some of the same tutors. Thomas Bayes died in 1761. After Bayes's death, the Bayes family asked Price to care for their father's papers, and Price came across an unpublished short essay on probability. Price did not finish adding to and editing the essay until 1763, when he sent his version of the original work under Bayes's name to the Royal Society. The original work by Bayes no longer exists, so how much of the paper accepted by the Royal Society was the original work of Bayes is unknown. In 1765, Price published another paper on the subject, this time in his own name, in which he improved and expanded on theories in the original essay submitted to the Royal Society. Some argue that what has become known as Bayes' theorem should be known as the Bayes-Price theorem.[11]

When Hume discussed the problem of induction, he was arguing from effect to cause. Hume thought there was no, or minimal, evidence of the effect (miracles), and therefore there was no basis for believing in the existence of the cause (God). Reasoning from effect to cause is known today as inverse probability.

Until Bayes' theorem, inverse probability was a seemingly intractable problem in mathematics. Before Price presented his paper to the Royal Academy, probabilities were calculated by reasoning from cause to effect, or what is known as forward probability. We toss a coin (the cause), and we know from our knowledge of coins that it will turn up either heads or tails (the effect). But let's assume we do not know whether the coin is fair. All we know is how many times it landed heads or tails. Bayes' theorem is a method of determining the odds that it is a fair coin. It allows us to compute inverse probabilities and thus, at least in Price's view, was a solution to the problem of induction.

Balls and Tables

In Bayes's writings, he did not take on Hume directly. Throughout his life, Bayes sought to avoid controversy, and that is perhaps why he never published his idea on how to calculate inverse probability. His consistent avoidance of the public spotlight also may explain why Bayes illustrated his method for determining inverse probabilities with an example of throwing two balls on a square table, a less contentious issue than miracles.[12]

In Bayes's example, our backs are turned to the table, and we cast the first ball over our shoulder onto the table. Our task is then to determine where on the table the first ball landed. To do so, an assistant hands us a second ball with which we conduct a similar throw. We then get a third ball and throw it, and so on. After each throw of a ball, the assistant tells us whether the ball landed on the near or far side of the first ball. Based on the evidence from the series of throws of many balls, we can estimate where the first ball is most likely to have landed.

For example, assume we conduct one hundred throws of additional balls, and we are told the balls landed on the near side of the first ball fifty times and on the far side the other fifty times. We can estimate that the first ball most likely landed in the middle of the table. Alternatively, suppose we are told that the additional balls always landed on the near side of the first ball. We should conclude that the first ball is probably at the far end of the table. Similarly, if we are told that the additional balls always landed on the far side of the first ball, then the first ball most likely landed at the near side of the table.

Bayes (or Price) wrote the following passage in the 1764 paper presented to the Royal Academy:

> *From the preceding proposition, it is plain that in the case of such an event as I there call M, from the number of times it happens and fails in a certain number of trials, without knowing any more concerning it, one may give a guess whereabouts it's [sic] probability is, and, by the usual methods of computing the magnitudes of the areas there mentioned, see the chance that the guess is right.*[13]

The event M referred to is evidence that the additional balls landed to the near or far side of the first ball. Before we cast additional balls, our estimate of where the first ball landed is called the prior.

Since our back is turned and we do not know where the first ball landed, our initial estimate, or prior, is that the first ball landed in the middle of the table. Suppose the toss of a second ball lands to the near side of the first ball. We should then revise the prior to reflect the new evidence that the first ball is likely closer to the far side of the table. This new estimate is called the posterior. We continually revise our estimate of where the first ball landed based on the evidence from subsequent throws that land to one side or the other of the first ball. After each throw of an additional ball, the posterior becomes the new prior, and the process repeats.

The preceding may seem obvious today, but this was a

revolutionary idea in the eighteenth century. Bayes' theorem was the first mathematical method proposed for induction, reasoning from effect to cause, or solving for inverse probability. In the example of the table, we do not know where the first ball landed but use the evidence of whether additional balls land on the near or far side of the first ball to estimate the first ball's position. Of course, the more throws of additional balls, the more confident we can be in our estimate. After one throw, we do not know much. After a hundred throws, we can be highly confident about where the first ball landed. Bayes' theorem shows us how to revise our beliefs based on new evidence.

Height and Racial Prejudice

We depend on inverse probability to make judgments in our everyday lives.

When walking down the street, we may seek to determine if the individual approaching is a threat. If we knew the person was a criminal intent on robbing us, then we would take evasive action. However, we often don't know their true intent until it is too late. Therefore, we judge the threat to person and property partly based on outward appearances. In this case, we are reasoning from effect (outward appearance) to cause (intent to hurt me).

One study showed that tall Black men were perceived to be more threatening than short Black men, but tall white men were believed to be less threatening than short white men.[14] The participants in this study did not know the intent of the men in question, but they inferred based on skin color and height that tall Black men posed a greater risk. If the participants had known the intent of the approaching individual, then they could have estimated the forward probability of being attacked. Because the intent of the approaching individual was unknown, the participants used skin color and stature to judge the threat posed by the individual.

The use of inverse probability would have revealed to the study participants their underlying prejudices. There is no evidence to support the view that criminality differs between races based on height.[15] Thus, after repeatedly encountering tall and short men of different races on the street, the study participants would soon realize that their biases were unfounded.

In this case, inverse probability can be used as a tool to counter conscious (or unconscious) prejudices about race and height by revising our initial beliefs based on additional evidence.

From Prejudice to Miracles

Price realized that Bayes' theorem offered a method to compute inverse probabilities and argue against Hume's skepticism about miracles. In an analogy to Bayes's table, the first ball represents an initial belief about the existence of God, and where the next balls land either confirms or refutes that belief. For example, we could assume that a subsequent ball landing on the near side of the initial ball represents evidence that God exists, such as miracles. Balls that land on the far side of the initial ball are evidence that God does not exist. The relative proportion of balls that land on either side of the initial ball is therefore our best estimate of the likelihood that God is real.

Although Price did not put forward specific numbers, he and other Christians acknowledged that miracles are exceptionally rare. (If commonplace, they would not be miracles.) Given the infrequency of miracles, we should not be surprised that most balls land on the far side of the initial ball. But that does not prove that God does not exist; it only proves that miracles are infrequent. Price believed Bayes' theorem proved that the low incidence of miracles was not inconsistent with the existence of God. In this way, Price sought to combine Hume's theories on induction with Bayes' theorem to refute Hume's critique of organized religion.

My read of Hume is that he was not, in fact, a committed atheist, despite what many of his contemporaries and later authors have written. Hume was nothing if not intellectually consistent, and thus I believe he thought the existence of God was possible but highly unlikely. Hume was fundamentally a skeptic, and the problem of induction led him to doubt the absolute certainty of any belief, including the claim that God did not exist. While Hume publicly was complimentary of the Bayes paper and Price's supplementary work, I suspect this was mainly due to his friendship with Price and a decision not to tarnish the reputation of the deceased Bayes.

Remarkably, there is no evidence that Hume recognized the importance of Bayes' theorem—no mention of it appears in Hume's writings. That was unfortunate, as Bayes' theorem is a powerful tool to solve many issues presented by the problem of induction.

Let's demonstrate with some examples.

But before we start, I should note that I am not going to present Bayes' theorem in the same way as every probability textbook I have read. If you are interested in the algebraic expression for Bayes' theorem, then you have bought (or borrowed) the wrong book. My other books about math contain no equations, and I am not starting now.

The reason is that I do not think about Bayes' theorem in equations. I prefer pictures in the form of decision trees.[16]

To illustrate, let's consider how to determine if a coin is fair.

Coins: Heads, Tails, and Fairness

If we toss a coin and it comes up heads or tails in equal numbers, then we conclude that the coin is likely fair. But if we toss a coin twice and it comes up heads both times, then what are the odds we are tossing an unfair coin?

To make the numbers easier, suppose there are two kinds of

coins in the world: those that are fair and those that are unfair, defined as always coming up heads. We can use Bayes' theorem in the form of a decision tree to determine the chances that our coin is unfair—that it has two heads.

Initially we do not know whether the coin is fair or unfair, so we assign an equal probability to each result. One way to think about this is to imagine a bag filled with equal numbers of fair and unfair coins, and we reach into the bag and pull out a coin at random. On the first and second flips of a fair coin, the results should be, on average, split evenly between heads and tails. On the first and second flips of an unfair coin, the outcome will be heads. We can then assign a probability to each of the potential outcomes of two flips of our coin of unknown fairness.

Figure 4.1

AN UNFAIR COIN: TWO HEADS

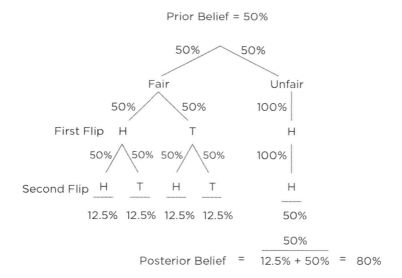

In this case, we are looking for the probability that the outcomes of the first and second flips were heads. In only two cases will both outcomes be heads: the 12.5 percent probability of two heads from the fair coin on the far left of the decision tree and the 50 percent chance from an unfair coin on the far right. This makes intuitive sense. We initially believed that half the coins in the bag were fair, and flipping a fair coin twice by Cardano's multiplication rule should yield two heads one-quarter of the time. We can expect half of one-quarter of the time (12.5 percent) to see two heads from the fair coin. Similarly, half of the coins in the bag were assumed to be unfair and land on heads 100 percent of the time. Half of 100 percent of the time (50 percent), we will see heads from an unfair coin.

The chance our coin is unfair can be estimated from the probability that an unfair coin is responsible for two heads (50 percent), divided by the probability of two heads, which is the sum of the probability of two heads from a fair coin (12.5 percent) and an unfair coin (50 percent). That equals 80 percent, or 50%/(12.5% + 50%).

Assume we toss the coin a third and fourth time and the results are also two heads. To calculate the odds our coin is unfair based on this additional information, we use our posterior belief from the results of the first two coin tosses as our new prior belief. In other words, we now estimate that there is an 80 percent chance the coin we drew out of the bag is unfair.

Figure 4.2

AN UNFAIR COIN: FOUR HEADS

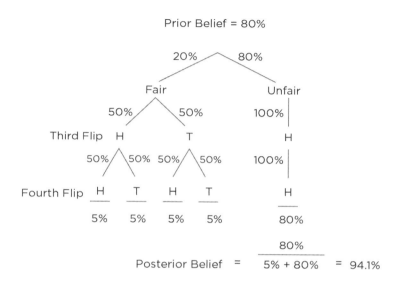

Once again, we are looking for the probability that the third and fourth outcomes are heads. In only two cases will both outcomes be heads: the probability of two heads from the fair coin on the far left (5 percent) and that from an unfair coin on the far right (80 percent).

The chances our coin is unfair can be estimated from the probability that an unfair coin is responsible for two heads (80 percent), divided by the probability of two heads, which is the sum of the probability of two heads from a fair coin (5 percent) and an unfair coin (80 percent). That equals 94.1 percent, or 80%/(5% + 80%). This is our new posterior belief based on the outcomes from four coin tosses yielding four heads.

We can continue this process indefinitely and, as the evidence mounts, gain a greater level of confidence in the fairness (or lack thereof) of our coin. Over time, the ratio of heads to tails might flip, and we may become convinced the coin is fair, or even biased toward tails. In any case, we should continually revise our estimate of the fairness of our coin based on the outcomes of each successive coin toss. As we have seen from this example of tossing a coin, the critical point is that Bayes' theorem is a mathematical means to quantify how to revise our beliefs based on new information.

Now let's turn to a real-world example of the use of Bayes' theorem: the COVID-19 test from the beginning of the book.

Medical Tests:
Don't Panic, the Doctor Calmly Said

In the Introduction, I gave an example of a medical test for COVID-19 that was 90 percent accurate. In other words, if you have the virus, then 90 percent of the time the test will come back positive and, if you do not, 90 percent of the time it will come back negative. It is assumed that in the patient's community one in one hundred people are infected.

To make the numbers easier, assume one thousand individuals are in the community. That means ten people (1,000 × 1%) have the disease and nine (10 × 90%) will test positive (true positive) and one (10 × 10%) will test negative (false negative). Out of the 990 (1,000 × 99%) patients who do not have the disease, 891 (990 × 90%) will test negative (true negative) and 99 (990 × 10%) will test positive (false positive).

Figure 4.3

COVID TEST #1

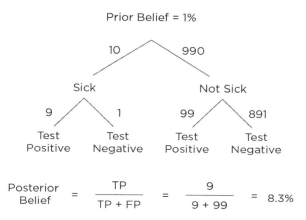

Prior Belief = 1%

$$\text{Posterior Belief} = \frac{TP}{TP + FP} = \frac{9}{9 + 99} = 8.3\%$$

The total number of positive cases is 108, or 9 true positives plus 99 false positives. If you test positive, the odds you have the disease are the number of true positives (9) divided by the total number of positives (108), or 8.3 percent.

We are confused by the odds because we fail to consider the low incidence of COVID-19 (one in one hundred individuals) within the community. Even a test that is highly accurate (90 percent) will produce a large number of false positives relative to true positives.

But this test result is still concerning because 8.3 percent is not zero. How do you determine whether you really have COVID-19? This is where the power of Bayes' theorem really comes into play. As in the example of the coin tosses, Bayes provides a means for us to revise our beliefs based on new information.

Based on the known prior of an incidence of the disease among all people, the doctor was able to estimate that the posterior probability that you are infected with the coronavirus, given a positive test result, is 8.3 percent. With that new information, we can retest and get a better estimate of the chances you have COVID-19.

Before the test, you were in a population of one thousand in which one in one hundred carried the coronavirus. After the test, you are in a population of 108 (the total number of true positives and false positives) in which the disease afflicts 9 (the number of true positives). Hence, we have a new prior incidence of COVID-19 in the patients who tested positive: 9 in 108, up from the initial 1 in 100.

Of those who tested positive in the first COVID-19 test, 9 people have the disease (true positives) and 99 do not (false positives). Let's round our numbers and assume in the second test of the 9 true positives that 8 test positive again (9 × 90%) and 1 tests negative (9 × 10%). Of the 99 who do not have the disease, 10 test positive (99 × 10%), and 89 test negative (99 × 90%).

Figure 4.4

COVID TEST #2

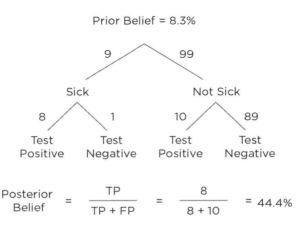

Prior Belief = 8.3%

$$\text{Posterior Belief} = \frac{TP}{TP + FP} = \frac{8}{8 + 10} = 44.4\%$$

The total number of positive cases is 18, or 8 true positives plus 10 false positives. The probability you have the disease if you test positive again is the number of true positives divided by the total number of positives, or 44.4 percent (8/(8+10)).

Testing a third time will give an even higher degree of certainty.

Figure 4.5

COVID TEST #3

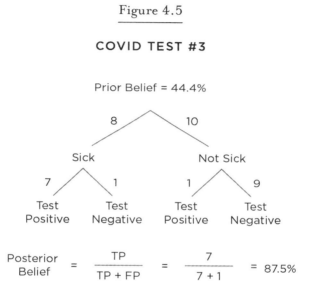

After a third positive test result, the chances you have COVID-19 are 87.5 percent. This is the power of Bayes' theorem: it shows us how to incorporate new information to arrive at better predictions, in this example to determine whether you are infected with the coronavirus.

Next, let's consider a real-life example of Bayes' theorem in action from the US military.

Submarines: The Bayesian Hunt for Red October

In 1984, Tom Clancy published his first book, *The Hunt for Red October*, a fictional account of a Soviet nuclear submarine whose captain and crew defect to the United States. A popular film based on the book followed in 1990. Clancy's debut novel, introducing the character of Jack Ryan, was inspired by the loss in 1968 of the Soviet submarine *K-129* and, weeks later, the USS *Scorpion*.

During the Cold War, and continuing to the present day, US and Soviet (now Russian) nuclear submarines play a deadly game of cat and mouse beneath the surface of the world's oceans. Modern submarines, once submerged, are difficult to detect and track. So, US and Russian submarines regularly hunt and follow each other at close range, which has resulted in several collisions.[17]

On March 8, 1968, the Golf-II class Soviet nuclear submarine *K-129* sank in the North Pacific. The Soviets launched a large-scale search and rescue operation but gave up after several months and declared all hands lost. On August 20, the USS *Halibut* identified the wreck of *K-129* northwest of Oahu, and the United States launched a CIA-led operation, code named Project Azorian, to recover the Soviet vessel. In a story worthy of a James Bond film, the CIA contracted with Howard Hughes to build a ship, the *Hughes Glomar Explorer*, that masqueraded as a vessel conducting deep sea mining for manganese. Instead, it really undertook a clandestine salvage of *K-129*. Exactly how much of *K-129* was recovered remains classified.

The speculation over why *K-129* went down continues to the present day. Among the reasons that have been put forward are a rogue crew, a hydrogen explosion from a defective battery, a missile malfunction, or a collision with the USS *Swordfish*. The US Navy has denied the latter. The CIA to this day has not disclosed what it knows.

Less than three months later, on May 22, 1968, the Skipjack

class nuclear submarine USS *Scorpion* sank off the coast of the Azores. Several books have been written alleging that the loss of the USS *Scorpion* was retaliation by the Soviets for the loss of *K-129*. The US Navy has denied this and, in a report released to the public, stated only that the USS *Scorpion* sank due to an unexplained explosion in one of the forward compartments.

But the conspiracy theories persist. In 1987, Peter Huchthausen, a now retired captain in the US Navy, asked Admiral Pitr Navoytsev, the first deputy chief of operations for the Soviet Navy, about the USS *Scorpion*.

The Soviet admiral replied: "Captain, you are very young and inexperienced, but you will learn that there are some things both sides have agreed not to address, and one is that event and our *K-129* loss, for similar reasons."[18]

Huchthausen followed up on that conversation in 1995 with retired Rear Admiral Viktor Dygalo, the former commander of the submarine division to which *K-129* had been assigned. Dygalo told him the true story will never be known due to an agreement between both navies. Dygalo said, "So forget about ever resolving these sad issues for the surviving families."[19] The *K-129* and the USS *Scorpio*n went down at the height of the Cold War. At that time, tensions between the two countries were high, and these events could have triggered a nuclear war.

Eight days after the USS *Scorpion* lost contact with the surface, the Navy declared the ninety-nine sailors aboard the nuclear submarine lost. The Navy then turned to Dr. John Craven, chief scientist in its Special Projects Office, to locate the missing sub.[20]

Craven had a history of finding things. Just two years earlier, in 1966, he located four hydrogen bombs that had dropped into the ocean off the coast of Spain after an American B-52 bomber collided with a refueling tanker. In that search and the one for the USS *Scorpion*, Craven employed a three-step Bayesian search process.

First, he determined the most likely places the sub would have settled across 140 square miles of ocean floor. He divided the area into a grid of cells, each with an alphanumeric code, such as B128 or S45. For each cell, experts then assigned probabilities that the sub was in the cell, based on nine potential scenarios such as a fire or Soviet attack.

Second, he calculated the search effectiveness of each cell in the grid as the product of the likelihood that the sub was in the cell and the searchers' ability to detect the wreckage if it was in that cell. The ocean floor has varying depths, and the deeper the water the less likely the wreckage of the sub could be detected by the Navy's cameras, sonars, and magnetometers. Based on the combination of these two factors, Craven picked a cell in which to start the search.

Third, based on the results of the search of a cell, he reestimated the initial prior probability of every cell on the grid and then started over again.

Craven was under tremendous pressure. President Lyndon B. Johnson required daily updates. The Navy's equipment was propelled underwater at a top speed of one knot per hour, and they had 140 square miles of ocean floor to cover. On October 28, forty-three days after the Navy began scanning the ocean floor, the wreckage of the USS *Scorpion* was found. It was a remarkable achievement.

Let's look at how Craven did it, using a simplified version of the Bayesian search for the USS *Scorpion*.

Instead of hundreds of cells, assume there are only two possible locations for the USS *Scorpion*: cells A and B. The experts believe the odds the sub went down within cells A and B are 60 percent and 40 percent, respectively. Further assume that the effectiveness of the Navy equipment for A and B are 10 percent and 80 percent, respectively. The sub is more likely to be in A. So, if we find the sub, what are the chances that it will be in A?

We use Bayes' theorem to calculate the answer.

Figure 4.6

HUNT FOR USS SCORPION

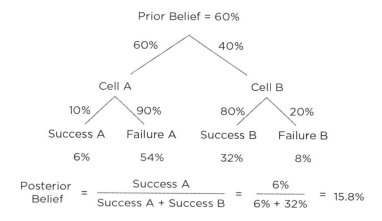

The chance of a successful search in A compared with B is the probability of finding the sub in A (6 percent, or 60% x 10%), divided by the probability of finding the sub in A (6 percent) plus the probability of locating the sub in B (32 percent, or 40% x 80%), or 15.8 percent. Even though the sub is more likely to be in A, there is a higher probability (84.2 percent) that we will successfully locate it in B. This is because the greater effectiveness of the Navy's equipment in detecting sunken subs in B outweighs the greater likelihood that the sub is resting in A.

Let's assume that our first search of B is a failure. Given that we did not find the sub in B, we reduce the likelihood that the sub is in B and then recalculate the chances that if we find the sub on the second search it will be in A. If the probability of finding the sub in A compared with B is still less than 50 percent, then we should once again search B. We continue to use the Bayesian search method until the sub is found, optimizing our limited search capacity each time.

In the case of the USS *Scorpion*, the US Navy was able to locate the sunken sub in record time. Today, the Bayesian search method is standard practice in locating missing aircraft and ships.

But the examples above are not the most frequently used applications of Bayes' theorem. For that, we turn to the online world.

Spam: Dirty Words and Clean Emails

Bayes' theorem is used millions of times per minute in spam filters throughout the world. Spam is a canned meat product and was famously repeatedly shouted, much to the dismay of the character played by Graham Chapman, in a three-minute 1970 Monty Python sketch. In the online world, spam refers to unwanted electronic messages. By one estimate, 85 percent of all emails sent today are spam.[21]

The first known instance of spam occurred in May 1864.[22] One Sunday evening, messenger boys from the District Telegraph Company delivered telegrams to well-known individuals throughout London. The telegrams were sent by a dodgy group of dentists, who marketed a tooth-whitening powder "used by Her Majesty."[23]

The telegram read:

> *Messrs. Gabriel, dentists, 27, Harley-street, Cavendish-square. Until October Messrs. Gabriel's professional attendance at 27, Harley-street, will be 10 to 5.*[24]

Given the relatively small number of telegrams sent, the first spam was unlikely to cause much of a rumpus or generate significant new sales of tooth-whitening powder. But several recipients of the unwanted telegrams posted angry letters to the London *Times*, which printed the letters and the offending telegram, generating free advertising for the clever dentists to a much larger audience.

Years later, the new technology of the telephone was also prone to unwanted electronic communications. In 1903, an elderly woman complained to the trade journal *Telephony* that her niece received a phone call from a male friend while dressing.

The upset aunt wrote: "The two of them stood talking to one another just as if they were entirely dressed and had stopped for a little chat on the street! I tell you this generation is too much for me."[25]

In terms of the online world, the first spam message is thought to be from Gary Thuerk, who on May 1, 1978, sent out an unsolicited mass emailing to four hundred customers over ARPANET, the first distributed, packet-switched electronic network, which evolved into today's internet.[26] Thuerk was the marketing manager for Digital Equipment Corporation and was hoping to garner sales for Digital's new T-series of VAX systems. The complaints began immediately, and an ARPANET representative called and made Thuerk promise never to do it again. But Thuerk's spam worked—it generated more than $13 million in sales of Digital's equipment.

Today, there is no representative from the internet to scold spammers. Instead, email providers have set up spam filters to block unwanted messages. These algorithms use Bayes' theorem to determine which emails are spam.

Spam filters come in many shapes and sizes. A common spam filter keys off specific words that are frequently used in unwanted emails. A 2018 survey listed the seven words most likely to trigger a spam filter: free, risk-free, click here, re: or fwd:, great offer, guarantee, and dear friend.[27]

To illustrate how spam filters work, assume the word "free" is contained in 20 percent of non-spam emails and 45 percent of spam emails. Also, suppose that spam emails are 25 percent of all emails. What are the odds an email containing the word "free" is spam?

Figure 4.7

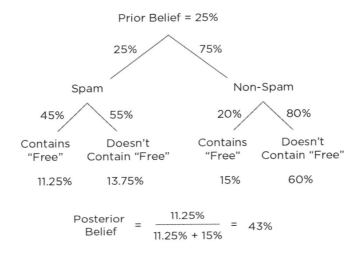

SPAM AND "FREE"

Forty-five percent of spam emails contain the word "free," therefore 11.25 percent (25% × 45%) of all emails contain the word "free" and are spam. We know that 20 percent of non-spam emails have the word "free," or 15 percent of all emails (75% × 20%). Therefore, if an email contains the word "free," there is a 43 percent chance (11.25%/(11.25% + 15%)) that it is spam.

Many words other than "free" are commonly associated with spam emails. The more words run through a spam filter, the greater the effectiveness, just as repetition improves the predictive value of medical tests or the search for submarines. Spam filters run Bayesian-based calculations on each word within an email. They also look at the originating email addresses and other information to help weed out junk mail. Regardless of the estimation criteria, the underlying methodology is based on Bayes' theorem.

Spam is a real problem. It is estimated that on an average day

122 billion spam emails are launched.[28] Advertising to generate sales is the leading category of spam emails (36 percent), followed by advertising adult sites (31 percent).[29] Contrary to popular belief, more spam emails originate from the United States, home to seven of the world's top ten spammers, than any other country.[30] Spam is estimated to cost American businesses and consumers about $20 billion every year on countermeasures and lost productivity.[31] Spam is illegal in the United States (CAN-SPAM Act of 2003). But that has not stopped spammers for two reasons: it is profitable, and it is hard to get caught.

Spammers generally do not market their own products. Instead, spammers typically sell leads to legitimate businesses. Because the cost of launching an email campaign is so low, spammers do not need much of a response rate to make money referring potential customers. One study estimated that a response rate of one in every 12.5 million emails was sufficient for spammers to earn thousands of dollars per day.[32] Spammers are difficult to locate because they often hijack a remote server, creating a "proxy bot," launch a spam campaign, and then jump onto another hijacked server.

Spammers have responded to spam filters with "Bayesian poisoning." Words can be classified in varying degrees of "spam-myness" (e.g., free) and "hammyness," (e.g., the). Spam filters estimate the probability that an email is spam based partly on the ratio of spammy to hammy words. In addition, words are assigned different weights. "Viagra" is given more weight than "free" in estimating spammyness. Similarly, "Charles Dickens" is given more weight than "the" in gauging hammyness. The ratio of the number of spammy to hammy words, weighted by the predictive value of a given word, is an important factor when determining whether an email is spam.

To poison a Bayesian filter, spammers flood their emails with common words and unusual phrases that are especially hammy.

Hence, you will sometimes see Charles Dickens referred to in an email about Viagra. In addition, spammers intentionally misspell words that a computer misses but a human has no trouble recognizing, such as "hundrd percnt mony makng sceme!"[33] Bayesian filters are effective but do not work as well when the inputs are corrupted.

Conclusions

The problem of induction, as formulated by David Hume, demonstrates that the best human reasoning process we can hope for is probabilistic conclusions. We believe the sun will rise tomorrow or that all right triangles adhere to the Pythagorean theorem, but both these statements ultimately rely on induction, which has some element of uncertainty.

Like Bayes tossing balls over his shoulder onto a square table, we can use Bayes' theorem to revise our beliefs based on additional information and become more confident in our conclusions. In the example of testing for the coronavirus, you could retest until some level of confidence that you are not infected is reached. Of course, there is a trade-off between the cost of gathering more information and the benefit of greater certainty. At some point, the effort and cost of taking another coronavirus test is not worth the additional assurance that you are disease-free. Fortunately, in many instances, decisions about that trade-off are within our control. Using Bayes' theorem, we can decide how much certainty we are willing to pay for.

Despite the power of Bayes' theorem, it was not widely used until the second half of the twentieth century. Many mathematicians disapproved of the theorem because the estimation of initial prior probabilities was considered "subjective."

In fact, the father of modern statistics completely rejected Bayes' theorem and refused to discuss it in his classes. But then again, he also believed that white people were genetically superior.

CHAPTER 5

Randomized Controlled Experiments: Not So Random

Ronald Fisher: Statistics and Improving the Human Stock

Ronald Fisher (1890–1962) was a British statistician, population geneticist, and a vocal proponent of eugenics who popularized the randomized controlled trial.[1] Fisher has been described as "the founder of modern statistical theory."[2]

Fisher was born in London, one of seven children. His mother died when he was just fourteen, and his father, an art auctioneer, lost his business a year later. Due to financial hardship, Fisher was awarded a scholarship to Cambridge, where he studied mathematics and graduated with distinction in 1912. After leaving Cambridge, he had no means of supporting himself and left

England to work on a farm in Canada. This was the beginning of Fisher's lifelong passion for agriculture. He returned to England and volunteered for the army at the outbreak of World War I, but he was rejected due to poor eyesight and ending up taking a job as a teacher.

In 1919, Fisher was offered a post as a statistician at the Rothamsted Experimental Station, the oldest agricultural research institute in the United Kingdom. His work at Rothamsted was the basis for many of his breakthroughs in probability and statistics. In 1925, he published *Statistical Methods for Research Workers*, which eventually went through fourteen editions and became the standard handbook for statistical analysis of scientific experiments for decades to come. In 1935, he followed up on that work with *The Design of Experiments*. In addition to his agricultural experiments, Fisher undertook tests for genetic fitness on mice, snails, and chickens and published the results in his book *The Genetical Theory of Natural Selection*.

In 1933, Fisher became a professor of eugenics at University College London. Ten years later, he returned to his alma mater to become the Arthur Balfour Professor of Eugenics at Cambridge University. He remained there until 1957 and then later relocated to Australia to lecture at the University of Adelaide, living out the last three years of his life down under.

Tax Incentives, Sterilization, and Nazis

Fisher had a keen interest in biology, even as a teenager, and read the works of Darwin, Galton, and Mendel. At Cambridge, Fisher cofounded the Cambridge University Eugenics Society.

As a third-year undergraduate, he gave a speech to the society titled "Mendelism and Biometry." He voiced his full support of eugenics during the talk, in which he emphasized how important it was for people to marry within their own social class—this would allow them to advance socially and materially. He was particularly concerned about the birth rates of the upper classes, those he considered to be superior: "There is no doubt that the birth-rate of the most valuable classes is considerably lower than that of the population in general."[3]

In *The Genetical Theory of Natural Selection*, published in 1930, Fisher expressed his conviction that throughout history an inverse relationship between class and fertility was responsible for a decline of nations. Fisher illustrated his beliefs by claiming the fall of the Roman Empire was partly due to a failure of leadership brought on by genetic degradation. He believed that the laws of inheritance applied to all animals, humans included; such laws covered physical properties, mental attributes, and moral attributes.[4]

To prevent what he saw as a similar fate befalling the United Kingdom, Fisher put forward two proposals. First, the UK government should use tax incentives to encourage upper-class families to have more children. Fisher thought such incentives would cover the standard-of-living differences between parents and non-parents and, as a consequence, would cause the standard of living to rise for those he deemed superior and to fall for those he thought inferior.[5] Second, the UK government should offer free voluntary sterilization to those suffering from "feeble mindedness" or "grave transmissible defects."[6] The UK authorities rejected both his proposals.

Even after World War II, when the horrors of Nazi Germany became common knowledge, Fisher continued to espouse eugenics and defend the worst of the field's practitioners. In 1947, the German geneticist Otmar Freiherr von Verschuer reached out to Fisher for a recommendation, as Verschuer's work for the Nazis was preventing him from gaining an academic post at the University of Frankfurt. From 1935 to 1942, Verschuer was director of the Institute for Genetic Biology and Racial Hygiene, which conducted "research" that the Nazis used as justification for the Holocaust. One of Verschuer's students was Josef Mengele, with whom Verschuer collaborated during World War II.

In his letter of recommendation for Verschuer, Fisher's sympathy with the Nazi eugenics program and Verschuer's actions was evident. He wrote approvingly of the Nazi Party's efforts to kill or sterilize people with mental disabilities and ascribed only positive and sincere motivations to those carrying out such directives.[7]

Fisher remained committed to a particularly racist branch of eugenics to the end of his life. In a response to a 1952 UNESCO report that discussed differences between races and nationalities, he (incorrectly) asserted that the available data provided a scientific basis for believing that different human groups had different intellectual and emotional capacities.[8] He went on to say that UNESCO ought to be concerned with the problem of how to deal with "persons of materially different nature."[9]

In 1954, in a letter to another professor, Fisher wrote that his and others' work in heredity "shows clearly what many of us have suspected—the vast differences in gene frequency existing between different human races."[10]

A Theory That Must Be Wholly Rejected

In addition to his beliefs concerning what he called "improving the human stock," Fisher was also a vehement opponent of the application of Bayes' theorem to problems that involve probability.[11] In his landmark 1925 book, *Statistical Methods*, there is no favorable mention of Bayes' theorem. On the contrary, Fisher wrote that "the theory of inverse probability is founded upon an error and must be wholly rejected."[12] Fisher believed that Bayes "reduces all probability to a subjective judgement."[13] That "subjective judgment" is the initial prior probability.

In the example of throwing balls on square tables, Bayes made an initial guess that the first ball landed in the middle of the table. Fisher was of the view that statistics should be based on "objective" facts, not "subjective" priors, which depended on the opinion of whoever set the initial prior. In circumstances in which the prior cannot be clearly deduced, Fisher believed Bayes' theorem not only had no value—it was misleading. He believed calculations that began with "subjective" priors, such as the first ball that lands in the middle of the table, invalidated Bayes' theorem. Those who share this antipathy toward Bayes' theorem are known as "frequentists," and Fisher was the leading proponent of this view.

But I think Fisher and the frequentists missed the point. Bayes and Price were not claiming that the prior is anything more than a guess and agreed that initial prior probabilities are often subjective. In our example of tossing a coin, if we knew the coin was fair, then there would be no need to test for fairness. It is because the prior is unknown that we compute inverse probability in the first place.

Furthermore, I believe no priors are truly objective anyway. Even deductive conclusions, such as those related to a coin toss, are based on inductive reasoning (see Chapter 4). Our intuitions may be right, but then again probability can mislead us. Scientists often have differing opinions about and approaches to testing a particular hypothesis. But after repeated and varied experiments, a consensus generally develops. On the other hand, frequentists hold firm convictions about what should happen, and when the unexpected arises, they often try to explain away an experimental outcome. In my view, it is better to rely on repeated trials using Bayes' theorem than preconceptions about the expected result.

We have discussed the example of the toss of a fair coin. Fisher claimed that over time the ratio of heads to tails will converge to 1:1. In an idealized world, that is true. But in the real world, I have argued there is no such thing as a truly random process, and an actual coin toss will tend to favor either heads or tails. But we cannot practically know down to a molecular level all the factors that determine the outcome to foresee on which side the coin is more likely to land. Hence, there is no way to "objectively" estimate the prior probable outcome of tossing a coin.

By contrast, we can determine the net effect of all these unknown factors through repeated trials and subsequent revisions of prior probabilities. The outcomes of coin tosses will converge toward an estimate of the sum of the imperfections in tossing mechanisms, tables, coins, etc. Regardless of the initial prior guessed by the experimenter, the results of an experiment involving coin tosses will push the experimenter toward the best estimate of whether a coin is fair. I may initially guess that a fair coin will land on heads all the time. But after repeated tosses I may have to revise my estimate.

In my view, intuition is less objective than an estimate arrived at after repeated experimentation. Intuition is helpful—but show me the data.

Unfortunately, prominent frequentists, led by Fisher, fought to keep Bayes' theorem out of mathematics and mainstream science. Fisher attacked the few mathematicians who argued in support of Bayes' theorem and "rendered it virtually taboo amongst respectable mathematicians."[14] A statistician during Senator Joseph McCarthy's anti-communist campaign in the 1950s called one of his coworkers "un-American because [he] was Bayesian and . . . undermining the United States Government."[15] One prominent mathematician wrote, "The laws of . . . Inverse Probability being dead, they should be buried out of sight, and not embalmed in test-books and examination papers . . . The indiscretions of great men should be quietly allowed to be forgotten."[16]

Fisher and other frequentists dominated academic statistics until the second half of the twentieth century. Fisher's antipathy toward Bayes' theorem was partly driven by his belief that there was only one valid methodology for making probabilistic statements in science.

He called it a randomized controlled trial.

Randomized Controlled Trials: The Gold Standard

More than any other statistician, Fisher is responsible for popularizing the randomized controlled trial (RCT), a method to estimate probabilities in science based on causal relationships. Others had used RCTs in psychology and education during the nineteenth century, but Fisher, through his research in agriculture and his books, convinced a generation of researchers across a wide variety of fields that RCTs were the "gold standard" for scientific studies.

In an RCT, subjects are randomly split into an experimental group that receives a treatment and a control group that is given either a placebo or no treatment at all. The outcomes of the experimental group are compared with the control group to determine the efficacy of the treatment. The objective of an RCT is to go beyond correlation to identify causal relationships. In effect, an RCT is just a way to test a counterfactual: if we do not give the treatment, then what are the consequences?

Comparing the outcomes from groups of individuals subject to different treatments is as old as the Bible. In 597 BC, King Nebuchadnezzar of Babylon was convinced by Daniel, a young man the king had enslaved, to run an experiment: feed only vegetables and water to Daniel and his friends while giving another group of boys access to the king's meat and wine.[17] (Ancient Babylon seems to have had relaxed rules concerning underage drinking.) After ten days, the king was so impressed with the significantly healthier appearances of Daniel and his friends that he made Daniel one of his most senior advisors. The experiment proved that Daniel's wisdom was "ten times better than all his magicians and astrologers that were in all his realm."[18]

However, as clever as Daniel might have been, he did not conduct an RCT. Daniel did not randomly pick the experimental group to be restricted to a vegetarian, teetotaler diet. By putting himself and his friends in one group, Daniel may have created two groups that were significantly different from one another. One might suspect that Daniel and his friends were either younger or healthier in appearance compared with the boys in the other group, who partook freely of the king's table. The key to an RCT is that the experimental and control groups are selected randomly to minimize the differences in the initial makeup of the two groups.

Equally important, randomization is thought to prevent the bias of the researchers from leaking into the study. Imagine that Daniel was more interested in the science than changing his status from an enslaved person to a senior advisor. In this case, Daniel would have tried to pick two groups with individuals who were comparable in physical appearance. However, even in this case, Daniel's judgment on outer beauty could contain unconscious biases that might skew the composition of the two groups. On the other hand, if Daniel picked the members of each group randomly, his biases would not affect the composition of the two groups of boys.

Tea and Manure

Fisher reported that he was first struck by the power of RCTs to estimate probabilities after preparing tea one afternoon in the late 1920s for a fellow biologist, Muriel Bristol, at the Rothamsted Experimental Station.[19]

Fisher had fixed a cup of tea for Bristol by pouring the milk first and then the tea. But Bristol refused to drink it because she said Fisher should have poured the tea first. Fisher was displeased and argued that she was being unreasonable. Fisher believed the order should not matter: adding A to B or adding B to A produced the same proportional mixture and temperature. But Bristol insisted she could taste the difference.

So, Fisher proposed an experiment.

In an adjacent room, Fisher prepared eight cups of tea: four with the milk poured first, and four with the tea poured first. He then brought them to Bristol to sample.

She correctly identified each one.

What Fisher and Bristol did not know at the time was that the order in which milk and tea are poured does make a difference. We know now that fats and proteins in milk react differently when they are initially surrounded by boiling water (pouring milk into tea) than when initially separated by a hot liquid (pouring tea into milk). Bristol did not know why, but she knew she could taste the difference.

Years later, Fisher reported that this experience drinking tea with a coworker was the inspiration for his work on experimental design and the development of procedures for RCTs. Although a good story, it is more likely Fisher's ideas were developed based on his work in the early 1920s in the fields of Rothamsted. In the ninety years before the arrival of Fisher, the scientists at Rothamsted had attempted to determine the best method for treating fields with manure. They would spread the fertilizer across an entire field and measure the potato yield at the harvest. This required adjusting for differing levels of rainfall year to year to make valid comparisons. In addition, each of the fields had varying soil composition, drainage, weeds, and so on. Despite decades of data, Rothamsted's agricultural scientists had failed to determine the optimal amount of manure to spread over a potato field.

In 1923, years before Fisher shared tea with his fellow biologist, Fisher and a colleague published "Studies in Crop Variation II."[20] In this paper, the authors analyzed the effect of fertilizer on potatoes at Rothamsted, but their method was completely different than that of their predecessors. Fisher and his coauthor randomly assigned different fertilizer treatments to the rows within each field. Fisher's idea was that the randomization of fertilizer treatments would compensate for differences within and between the characteristics of the fields. He could also test the effectiveness of the treatments within one growing season, without the difficulties of correcting for weather from one year to the next. By randomizing his samples, Fisher believed he could prove a causal link between specific fertilizer treatments and potato crop yields. In fact, Fisher accomplished what he set out to achieve. He became the first scientist at Rothamsted to provide solid evidence on the effectiveness of various types and levels of manure.

Based on his success at Rothamsted, Fisher became convinced that only RCTs could reliably estimate the probability that a given cause (e.g., manure) would yield a particular effect (e.g., potato yield). Consequently, Fisher and many generations of statisticians to follow viewed RCTs as the gold standard of scientific experimentation.

One reason Fisher and others dismissed scientific studies without randomization is that they believed such studies were infected by the biases of the researchers. One example of this type of bias can be found in studies on the effectiveness of acupuncture.

The ancient practice of acupuncture is widely accepted in many Asian countries but often viewed with a degree of skepticism in the rest of the world. In one survey of forty-seven studies of acupuncture conducted in China, Taiwan, and Japan between 1966 and 1995, all had concluded that the treatment was effective.[21] During the same period, in ninety-four clinical trials of acupuncture in the United States, Sweden, and the United Kingdom, only 56 percent of these studies found therapeutic benefits.[22] The authors of the survey wrote that "scientists find ways to confirm their preferred hypothesis, disregarding what they don't want to see."[23]

Girolamo Cardano (1501–1576) was a mathematician, physician, and astrologer who wrote the first treatise on probability. His work on probability arose from his lifelong addiction to gambling. *Reproduced by permission. © Pictorial Press Ltd /Alamy Stock Photo*

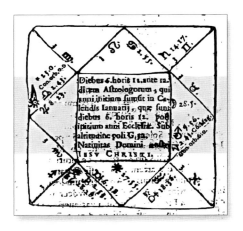

The horoscope of Christ or "Jesus Natal Chart. 25 Dec 0001 BC, Bethlehem," as cast by Cardano. This horoscope foretells a bright comet at Christ's birth, signifying future greatness, and the warlike planet Mars in opposition to the moon, indicating a violent death. *Source: https://www.academia.edu/27310724/ An_Unusual_Biography_Cardanos_Horoscope_of_Petrarch*

Let's Make a Deal was a popular TV game show in which a valuable prize was hidden behind one of three doors. In theory, a contestant should always switch after the host revealed a "zonk" behind one of the doors. In practice, the host often offered contestants additional cash not to switch. Hence, the odds did not always favor switching. *Source: https://course-studies. corsairs.network/understanding-the-monty-hall-problem-a40f7d5a0e4d*

Johann Gauss (1777–1855) was a mathematician and physicist who invented the normal distribution, the most commonly used probability distribution today. Gauss amassed a sizeable fortune through shrewd investing and was one of the most celebrated scientists of his time, although his personal life was by marked by tragedy. *Reproduced by permission.* © *GL Archive/Alamy Stock Photo*

Benoit Mandelbrot (1924–2010) was a mathematician best known for his work in geometry. Mandelbrot questioned the use of normal distributions in the social sciences. His work in probability was largely ignored for five decades until the financial crisis of 2008–2009. *Photo © 2010 by Steve Jurvetson. https://commons. wikimedia.org/wiki/File:Benoit_Mandelbrot,_TED_2010.jpg*

David Hume (1711–1776) was a philosopher, historian, and economist and considered the greatest of the British Empiricists. A proponent of American Independence and opponent of organized religion, Hume was widely criticized by his contemporaries but significantly altered the course of modern philosophy by demonstrating the limitations of human reasoning, or what has become known as the Problem of Induction. *Reproduced by permission. © GL Archive / Alamy Stock Photo*

Thomas Kuhn (1922–1996) was a philosopher of science who pioneered the idea of paradigm shifts in human knowledge. Kuhn compared the structure of scientific revolutions to evolution, in which worldviews are resistant to change until challenged by overwhelming evidence. *Copyright © Jane Reed. From University Archives, Sheridan Libraries, Johns Hopkins University.*

Karl Popper (1902–1994) was a philosopher who wrote several best-selling books on politics and science. Popper believed science progressed through critical rationalism, the belief that a scientific theory can never be conclusively proven, only falsified. *Reproduced by permission. Photograph © by Steve Pike. Getty Images*

Richard Price (1723–1791) was a philosopher, mathematician, and political scientist. He is known today for uncovering and developing Bayes' theorem after discovering a method to compute inverse probability in the papers of his deceased friend. Among the most widely read church leaders of his day, Price believed Bayes' theorem offered a solution to Hume's Problem of Induction and a means to rebut the arguments advanced by atheists. *Source: Portrait of Dr. Richard Price by Benjamin West. The National Library of Wales.*

[370]

quodque folum, certa nitri figna præbere, fed plura
concurrere debere, ut de vero nitro producto dubium
non relinquatur.

LII. *An Eſſay towards ſolving a Problem in
the Doctrine of Chances. By the late Rev.
Mr. Bayes, F. R. S.* communicated by Mr.
Price, *in a Letter to* John Canton, *A. M.
F. R. S.*

Dear Sir,

Read Dec. 23, 1763.   I Now ſend you an eſſay which I have
found among the papers of our de-
ceaſed friend Mr. Bayes, and which, in my opinion,
has great merit, and well deſerves to be preſerved.
Experimental philoſophy, you will find, is nearly in-
tereſted in the ſubject of it; and on this account there
ſeems to be particular reaſon for thinking that a communication of it to the Royal Society cannot be im-
proper.

He had, you know, the honour of being a member of that illuſtrious Society, and was much eſteem-
ed by many in it as a very able mathematician. In an
introduction which he has writ to this Eſſay, he ſays,
that his deſign at firſt in thinking on the ſubject of it
was, to find out a method by which we might judge
concerning the probability that an event has to happen, in given circumſtances, upon ſuppoſition that we
know nothing concerning it but that, under the ſame
                                                circum-

A reprint of the first page of a letter sent in 1793 by Price to John Canton, a member of the Royal Society, recommending an essay written by "our deceased friend Mr. Bayes." In subsequent pages, Price recounts how Bayes provided a "solution of the inverse problem." There is no record of the original Bayes' essay. *Source: The Royal Society Publishing. https://royalsocietypublishing.org/doi/10.1098/rstl.1763.0053*

The Glomar Explorer, part of Project Azorian, a secret US government operation to salvage the sunken Soviet submarine *K-129*. The CIA contracted Howard
Hughes to build a ship that could masquerade as a deep-sea mining vessel while
raising *K-129* from the ocean floor. *U.S. Government Photo. http://www.gwu.
edu/~nsarchiv/nukevault/ebb305/index.htm*

Soviet ballistic missile submarine *K-129* (722), containing two nuclear war-heads, on patrol in the Pacific during the 1960s. During August of 1974, the Glomar Explorer successfully lifted wreckage from *K-129* and the bodies of Soviet sailors to the surface. The CIA report of what was found remains classified. *Official CIA Photograph. https://commons.wikimedia.org/wiki/ File:Soviet_ballistic_missile_submarine_K-129.jpg*

The wreck of the USS *Scorpion* (SSN-589) on the ocean floor, 400 miles southwest of the Azores. Several former senior US Naval officers have alleged that the USS *Scorpion* was attacked in retaliation for the sinking of the Soviet sub *K-129* three months earlier. The US Navy has denied this claim. Official U.S. Navy photograph, from the collections of the Naval History and Heritage Command. *https://www.history.navy.mil/content/history/nhhc/our-collections/photography/numerical-list-of-images/nhhc-series/nh-series/NH-97000/NH-97223-KN.html*

TO THE EDITOR OF THE TIMES.

Sir,—On my arrival home late yesterday evening a "telegram," by "London District Telegraph," addressed in full to me, was put into my hands. It was as follows :—

"Messrs. Gabriel, dentists, 27, Harley-street, Cavendish-square. Until October Messrs. Gabriel's professional attendance at 27, Harley-street, will be 10 till 5."

I have never had any dealings with Messrs. Gabriel, and beg to ask by what right do they disturb me by a telegram which is evidently simply the medium of advertisement? A word from you would, I feel sure, put a stop to this intolerable nuisance. I enclose the telegram, and am,

Your faithful servant,

Upper Grosvenor-street, May 30.   M. P.

A letter to the editor of *The London Times* complaining of an unwanted telegram sent by Messrs. Gabriel. This is the first known instance of an unsolicited electronic communication designed to sell a service or product, or what today is known as spam. The effectiveness of this first spam message was greatly enhanced by subsequent letters to the editor by angry recipients. *Source: https://blog.adaptivemobile. com/blog-spam-day-2016*

Sally and Stephan Clark appearing before the media upon Sally's release from jail after winning an appeal against her conviction for the murder of their two sons. Sally would later commit suicide after battling depression. *Reproduced by permission.* © *GL Archive REUTERS/Alamy Stock Photo.*

Ronald Fisher (1890–1962) was a statistician, geneticist, and a vocal proponent of eugenics. In a series of books, Fisher popularized randomized controlled trials as the "gold standard" of scientific experiments and argued that studies linking ciga-rette smoking and lung cancer were "propaganda." *Reproduced by permission.* © *GL Archive / Alamy Stock Photo*

Fisher in Confederate garb at a gathering in Blue Ridge, North Carolina. Fisher believed there were "vast differences" in the genetics of various races. He wrote that governments should incentivize the rich to have more children and the "feebleminded" to be voluntarily sterilized. After WWII, he continued to recommend former Nazis doctors involved in the Holocaust for academic posts. *Source: https://thisviewoflife.com/ronald-fisher-is-not-being-cancelled-but-his-eugenic-advocacy-should-have-consequences/*

A 1930s poster distributed by the Eugenics Education Society of London (EESL). Ronald Fisher was a board member of EESL and active in the Committee for Legal Sterilization. Fisher wrote a four-page pamphlet for the committee entitled, "The Elimination of Mental Defect," in which he claimed as justification for his proposals that, "defectives undoubtedly gravitate to the lowest social stratum." *Source: https://thisviewoflife.com/ronald-fisher-is-not-being-cancelled-but-his-eugenic-advocacy-should-have-consequences/*

Barbara Burks (1902–1943) was a psychologist who published in her short career more than 80 articles and books. She pioneered the use of causal diagrams in the social sciences and conducted breakthrough research in genetics. But she was never able to gain a professorship or senior research position in the male-dominated field of psychology of the 1930s and 1940s. She committed suicide at 40 years of age. *Source: https://www.gf.org/fellows/all-fellows/barbara-s-burks/*

In 1921, Burks was one of the first women granted a commercial wireless operator's license, which required passing numerous technical tests and mastering Morse code. She is shown here behind the microphone of the University of California Station 6BB in Berkeley, California. *Source: www.paara.org/newsletter/2021/graph0121.pdf*

In the case of Daniel and the king, Fisher would have been convinced that a vegetarian, alcohol-free diet was superior only if Daniel had picked the members of the two groups randomly. However, Fisher would not have been persuaded if Daniel simply presented evidence that Daniel and his friends appeared healthier.

But in my view, the benefits of randomization in controlled trials are not as straightforward as Fisher believed.

Random Is Not Necessarily Random

One of the basic assumptions that Fisher made about RCTs was that a sufficiently large number of trials are run so that the differences between the experimental and control groups average out over time. But this is often not the case.

Let's return to Fisher's experiments in manure treatments at Rothamsted. Assume there are only two fields, North and South. Assume Treatment 1 is randomly assigned to North and Treatment 2 to South, and the results of this experiment show that the two treatments are equally effective at growing potatoes.

But suppose that the soil in North is more fertile.

A researcher relying only on randomization will incorrectly conclude on the basis of a single RCT that the efficacy of the two treatments is the same, even though Treatment 2 is superior, given that it yielded similar amounts of potatoes from a less fertile field. On the other hand, if the researcher undertakes one hundred RCTs, each time randomly assigning treatments to either North or South, then it will become clear over time that Treatment 2 is more effective.

Unfortunately, many RCTs can be run only infrequently. As a practical matter, we often cannot repeatedly conduct studies over long time periods, such as cancer studies that often span ten or twenty years. Consequently, the effectiveness of a cancer drug may be simply a function of the differences between the experimental and control groups in an RCT. In the same way the North field is more fertile than the South field, the experimental group may be more receptive to the drug than the control group.

A recent survey of the ten most-cited RCT studies concluded that the composition of the experimental and control groups of these trials was not so random after all.[24] The authors of this study wrote that "researchers in fields like medicine, psychology and economics often claim that [RCTs are] the only reliable means to properly inform medical, social and policy decisions."[25] However, the authors discovered this claim was inconsistent with the outcomes from these RCT studies.

The most commonly cited RCT on strokes reported that mortality at three months was 20 percent lower in the treatment group compared to the control group. However, it was later determined that those who received the treatment were 8 percent less likely to have been smokers and 14 percent more likely to have been taking aspirin therapy. The largest RCT concerning chemotherapy and breast cancer concluded that the treatment group survived 4.5 months longer than the control group. However, the treatment group was 16 percent more likely to have received the treatment before the start of the study, and the response to chemotherapy can be less effective when exposed to the treatment for the first time. The higher survival rate of the treatment group could simply be a function of an earlier exposure to the treatment.

Based on biases found in the ten most-cited RCT studies, the authors concluded that if researchers focus on randomly distributing participants rather than "systematically ensuring participants are distributed well at baseline and endline, then scientific understanding will be undermined in the name of computer-based randomization."[26]

When randomly dividing subjects into experimental and control groups, Fisher assumed that the differences between the two would cancel each other out. This is often not true. The alternative, which Fisher rejected as too subjective, is for the researcher to adjust outcomes based on other factors. In the case of potatoes and manure, the researcher could test the soils of the North and South fields and discount the yields from the North field to account for its greater fertility.

Fisher was adamantly against this approach, as he believed it introduced the biases of the experimenter into the experiment. The experimenter, for example, may prefer certain types of soils for growing potatoes based on experiences in years past and unconsciously discount the fertility of one of the fields. Fisher argued that only randomization assured that experiments are freed from researchers' preconceptions. However, we have seen that random is not necessarily random, particularly when the number of trials is limited. Randomization does protect an experiment from researcher bias. But that comes at a cost: we can sometimes end up with significant differences between experimental and control groups.

The critical question is which approach reduces the differences between experimental and control groups: eliminating unconscious bias or adding conscious selection. The trade-off between randomization and purposeful selection depends on the facts and circumstances of each experiment.

This is particularly true for many clinical trials of drugs conducted today.

Success Favors the Unrepresentative

In an RCT to determine the effectiveness of a medicine, patients are randomly divided into experimental and control groups. The former is given the drug, and the latter is given either no treatment or a placebo.

Suppose a drug is designed to cure a certain type of cancer. Assume the drug is totally ineffective and half the population has a "cancer gene," which makes a person more susceptible to die from this type of cancer. Eight teams of researchers conduct eight separate studies. For simplicity, and to make the numbers easier, we will stipulate that three patients are selected for each study, and a given patient has a 50:50 chance of having the cancer gene.

This example is comparable to conducting an experiment to determine the probability that a fair coin will land on tails three times in a row. When conducting such an experiment, we expect that one out of every eight trials on average will produce three consecutive tails (1/2 × 1/2 × 1/2 = 1/8). Similarly, in one of the eight trials of our medical experiment, we expect that three individuals without the cancer gene will constitute all three patients that receive the drug in the trial. In that trial, our ineffective cancer drug will be shown to be more effective. In the other seven trials, our ineffective drug will demonstrate no or limited efficacy. Only the one unrepresentative trial in which all the individuals lack the cancer gene will "prove" the drug is effective and be declared a success.

Medical journals typically publish only the results of trials that demonstrate successful positive outcomes. A medical experiment that shows a drug does not work is considered of no value to patients and is rarely accepted. (If you wish to dive deeper into this type of publication bias in the medical field, see my book *Fooled by the Winners*.) In our example, only one of the eight trials is likely to see the light of day; the others will be filed in a lab drawer with the label "Results Inconclusive." Hence, some RCTs will "prove" a drug is effective, when the real reason for the result is the difference between the experimental and control groups. The only way to minimize this danger is for researchers to consciously divide groups based on known characteristics. In other words, researchers should place an equal number of individuals with and without the cancer gene in each trial.

Those who believe, like Fisher, that RCTs are the only valid methodology for scientific experiments argue that sometimes the underlying characteristics of groups are unknown. In the preceding example, we may not be able to detect the presence of the cancer gene in the subjects of our experiment. However, as a practical matter, the characteristics of most populations are measurable. In the case of medical trials, we know about such things as age, sex, income, preexisting conditions, history of illness, etc.

In my opinion, adjusting for known characteristics is better than randomization. Admittedly, it is a trade-off: the luck of the draw versus the unconscious biases of the drawer. But I would rather rely on the skill of a researcher to sort the experimental and control groups, even given the potential for researcher bias, than depend on a random number generator.

An analogy is an attempt to reproduce Act I of *Hamlet*. With enough time at a typewriter, a person could randomly strike the keys and produce the words written by the Bard. Alternatively, a person could try to recall Act I from memory and tap out a rough approximation. The former would be unbiased: eventually, the beginning of Shakespeare's play will be typed out, word for word. The latter will be biased: the memory of the person at the typewriter will not be perfect, and the pages will omit some passages and add others. But while the latter will not be an exact reproduction, it will be a lot closer to the original over any reasonable amount of time.

Unfortunately, Fisher's views on RCTs and a strict adherence to randomization have become a matter of blind faith for many researchers. These same researchers disregard the conclusions of nonrandomized studies as unscientific due to the role of the scientist in selecting the sample populations. Of course scientists have biases. However, I do not see how leaving the composition of the experimental and control groups up to chance is necessarily a better answer.

Therefore, I do not believe we should draw such a sharp

distinction between RCTs and nonrandomized studies. We should approach both with a degree of skepticism. Neither RCTs nor nonrandomized studies are without flaws. We would be better off considering the strengths and weaknesses of RCTs and nonrandomized studies and selecting the most appropriate method for a given study.

This reliance on RCTs as the gold standard for scientific experiments is part of the reason for what is known today as the replication crisis.

It Definitely Worked Once

Public recognition that science has a replication crisis began in 2005 with the publication in *PLOS Medicine* of an essay titled "Why Most Published Research Findings Are False" by John Ioannidis, a professor of medicine at Stanford University.[27]

In his essay, Ioannidis stated that "it can be proven that most claimed research findings are false."[28] He went on to assert that this was because of the common practice of relying on the results of a single study.[29]

Ioannidis cautioned that "it is misleading to emphasize the statistically significant findings of any single team. What matters is the totality of the evidence."[30] He based this warning on a survey of the most-cited epidemiological studies that showed five of the six studies had been fully contradicted or been found to have exaggerated their results.[31]

Others have reached similar conclusions. An internal study by the firm Amgen reviewed fifty-three "landmark studies" in biotechnology and found the findings in these papers were confirmed in only 11 percent of cases.[32] A team at Bayer reported that only 25 percent of published preclinical cancer studies could be validated to the point at which it was worth further investigating the effectiveness of the treatment.[33] Another study concluded that $28 billion is spent each year in the United States on drug research that cannot be replicated.[34] In a recent survey by *Nature* of 1,576 researchers, "more than 70 percent of researchers have tried and failed to reproduce another scientist's experiments and more than half have failed to reproduce their own experiments."[35] The majority of those surveyed believed there was a "crisis of replicability."[36]

Several reasons have been put forth to explain the replicability crisis in science.

One reason is misconduct by researchers, which has been reported by the media. However, it is estimated that outright fraud or significant misrepresentation constitutes only a small portion of the published research that has subsequently been proven to be wrong.[37] Another reason sometimes cited is the proliferation of scientific studies. The total number of registered clinical studies worldwide rose from 100,208 in 2010 to 362,524 in 2020.[38] While the number of clinical studies has tripled, it is not clear whether the number of productive experiments to be run—and enough qualified experimenters to run them—has also increased. The replication crisis could be caused by an overall decline in opportunities for fruitful research and the quality of the experiments. However, the largest and most-cited studies also suffer from a replication crisis. Of the forty-five most frequently cited studies that claimed a treatment was effective, only 44 percent could be replicated.[39]

A more commonly given reason for the replication crisis is publication bias. In psychology, the proportion of published results that are statistically significant exceeds 90 percent.[40] In neuroscience, that number is 85 percent, and in animal sciences it is 78 percent.[41] It seems highly unlikely that such a high percentage of experiments would yield statistically significant positive results. These higher numbers are probably due to publication bias within scientific journals that have little interest in publishing an inconclusive outcome.

Publication bias is real and endemic to scientific journals. However, I believe it is just a symptom of the underlying disease. If an experiment yields a statistically significant finding, then the researchers naturally strive to get it published to further their careers. If an experiment produces an inconclusive result, then the results of that experiment are often buried in a file drawer and never looked at again. But a statistically significant finding can simply be the result of an RCT in which the experimental and control groups happened to differ. These differences, and not the effectiveness of the treatment, may often account for a positive result.

I believe few scientists consciously lie. Most researchers are fairly reporting the outcomes of their experiments. They just keep trying RCTs until they get a positive outcome.

As we have seen, a random process will eventually yield what appears to be a nonrandom result, the equivalent of tossing a fair coin and having heads coming up three times in a row. Repeating the same RCT enough times will eventually produce experimental and control groups with different characteristics that can lead to a statistically significant positive outcome, even if the treatment is ineffective.

In our example, a researcher could conduct enough RCTs that an experimental group will eventually arise that has patients without the cancer gene. This RCT will incorrectly conclude that the drug is effective at curing cancer. But when the next RCT is undertaken with a more representative group in which a portion of the population possesses the cancer gene, the original study will not be replicated.

Conclusions

Replication of experimental results is at the heart of the scientific process. It is what separates science from religion, in which beliefs are strictly personal and not subject to independent confirmation by others.

The late John Maddox, the legendary editor of the leading scientific journal *Nature*, was asked how much of what appeared in his magazine would eventually turn out to be wrong. He replied, "All of it."[42] Maddox understood that the advancement of science depended on the verification of experimental results by others, and that over time new theories would replace the old. But if neither old nor new theories can be verified, then there can be no scientific progress.

One of the main causes of today's crisis of replication is a blind belief in RCTs as the gold standard of scientific experimentation. In many experiments, the randomly selected subjects are not so random.

For many years, determining how experiments were affected by nonrandom factors, such as differences between control and treatment groups, was an inexact science. That was the case until one of the pioneers in twentieth-century psychology demonstrated a method for identifying the causes of these differences.

But because this pioneer was a woman, she never received the recognition she was due. And she took on Ronald Fisher.

CHAPTER 6

Causality:
A Diagram Is Worth
a Thousand Words

Barbara Stoddard Burks:
Pioneer in the Social Sciences

Barbara Stoddard Burks (1902–1943) was an American psychologist who invented several ground-breaking statistical methods.[1] In her brief career, she published more than eighty articles and books in developmental and educational psychology as well as genetics. She was the first person known to have drawn a causal diagram in the social sciences. As a prominent statistician wrote, Burks's use of path analysis "was decades ahead of its time."[2]

Burks was born in New York to an academic family. Her father was a well-known scholar in the field of educational research, and her mother was an author of textbooks and popular children's novels. Both her father and mother were from prominent American families: her father was descended from the earliest settlers of Virginia, and her mother was descended from Jonathan Edwards and Benjamin Franklin.

During World War I, the family moved to Washington, DC. After graduating from high school at sixteen, Burks went to work as a statistician for the National Bureau of Standards. Several years later the family moved again, this time to California, and Burks enrolled at the University of California, Berkeley. She transferred to Stanford University in her senior year to study with Lewis Terman, one of the leading educational psychologists of his time.

Terman was extremely impressed with the college senior and later wrote:

> *The unusual quality of her mind was so immediately evident that she was advised at once to proceed to the doctorate without undergoing the usual probationary period before setting this goal. Her record as a graduate student was in fact one of the best I have ever known.*[3]

Burks was Terman's research assistant from 1924 to 1930, and she earned a PhD in psychology from Stanford in 1929, a highly unusual feat at that time for the male-dominated profession.

As a woman, Burks found jobs in academia scarce, and after graduation, she took a job as a school psychologist in Pasadena. She had married Herman Ramsperger, a professor of chemistry at the California Institute of Technology, in 1927, but he was diagnosed with terminal lung cancer in 1931 and died the next year. Burks moved back to the Bay Area and worked as a research assistant at the University of California, Berkeley. In recognition of her previous work with Terman, Burks was awarded a fellowship in

Europe and spent seven months collaborating with Carl Jung in Zurich and Jean Piaget at the Rousseau Institute in Geneva.

After returning from Europe, Burks took a job at the Carnegie Institute in New York. She also served as editor for a leading journal of psychology. However, despite her pioneering academic research and active involvement in the field, the gender divide in the labor market for psychology PhDs constrained her career options.

A survey of psychology departments of American universities and research labs around the time of World War II presented the following conclusions:

> *Male Ph.D.s tended to hold high-status jobs in university and college departments, concentrating on teaching and experimental research. Female Ph.D.s, on the other hand, were usually tracked into service-oriented positions in hospitals, clinics, courts, and schools. Discouraged and frequently prevented from pursuing academic careers, women filled the ranks of applied psychology's low-paid, low-status workers.*[4]

Burks felt the sting of gender discrimination throughout her career. After accepting another research assistant position, she wrote in a February 14, 1939, letter to Terman, "Of course I would welcome an invitation from a university with a good department of psychology. . . . There is no instructional program here, and there are no other psychologists here."[5]

Burks was never able to obtain a professorship or senior research position. During the late 1930s, she began to suffer from deep depressions. In 1942, she became engaged to a colleague, Robert Cook, which seemed to improve her mental state. But it was not enough. On the evening of May 25, 1943, she walked onto the George Washington Bridge in New York City and fell to her death.[6] She was forty years old.

On June 7, in a letter to the *New York Times*, a coworker wrote that "the sudden death last week of Dr. Barbara Stoddard Burks will be keenly felt by her scientific colleagues in psychology and genetics as well as by others who have followed her interesting work in human society and the influence of environment."[7]

Burks was the first in the social sciences to set out a systematic method, involving causal graphs, to separate cause from effect in observational studies. This can be illustrated by the apparent connection between ice cream and drowning.

Correlation Is Not Causation

In the United States, there is a statistically significant positive correlation between the monthly sales of ice cream and the incidence of drowning deaths. Swimmers burn calories and are often hungry for high-calorie nourishment afterward. But the real reason for this positive correlation is that sales of ice cream and the incidence of swimming both rise during the summer.

In previous chapters, I have argued that induction is the basis of all reasoning, and therefore all conclusions should be couched in terms of probability. While A may have been associated with B in the past, that does not mean it will always be so in the future. Our confidence that A and B will be bound together going forward depends on numerous factors, including how tightly bound they were in the past and the uniformity of conditions through time. Even though there is no causal relationship between the two, the incidence of ice cream consumption and drownings have closely tracked each other historically. However, this correlation is not sufficient to demonstrate causality.

Some empiricists and statisticians are skeptical that we can prove a causal relationship between events. They believe human reasoning is limited to association: we can only know with certainty that two events regularly occur together, and no more. They argue we are fooled into believing A causes B based on a lifetime of experiences in which A and B coincided.

Most empiricists and statisticians, however, do believe that we can prove that causal relationships exist. But there are differences of opinion on how to do that.

In my opinion, counterfactuals are the key.

Counterfactuals: The Basis of Causality

When we say A causes B, we do not mean that A and B merely occur together regularly. We mean that (1) A and B occur together regularly and (2) A is sufficient but not necessary for B to occur. In other words, A is one possible cause of B.

The second condition is the counterfactual claim that separates causality from correlation. To demonstrate correlation, we only need prove the first condition, that in the past B has been associated with or followed by A. To show causation, we must prove both conditions—that A and B occur together, and without A or some other cause, B will not occur. For example, sunrises and the crows of roosters are correlated. While a sunrise is a sufficient condition for crowing, it is not necessary. Roosters squawk throughout the day, so a sunrise is not required for these birds to vocalize. The second condition is the counterfactual claim that on a day without a sunrise (and no other causes), roosters will not crow.

In addition, before demonstrating causality, we should specify a given set of conditions. The sun rising is sufficient cause for the rooster to crow, assuming the rooster has enough oxygen to take a breath, food to expend the energy to crow, and other prerequisites for squawking. Once these other conditions are established, we can demonstrate a causal link between sunrises and loud bird noises.

To prove causality, we must engage in counterfactual reasoning since no human has experienced a day without a sunrise. This ability to reason in terms of counterfactuals is part of what separates us from other living organisms and makes us human. To go beyond induction based on experience requires imagining a sequence of events that has never happened. To the best of our knowledge, animals do not think in terms of counterfactuals. Animals associate gestures or voice commands with the provision of food by humans, and so they are trainable. But animals have not taken the next step to imagine a world in which they train humans by offering them treats. Armed with a brain that can process counterfactuals, humans have vanquished other animals and are the dominant species on the planet. The ability to think in terms of counterfactuals is an important part of why we dine on Chinese takeout in skyscrapers and monkeys chow down on bananas in zoos.

Nevertheless, we are often misled about the likelihood of an event occurring in the future, even though we are equipped with a counterfactually enabled brain. Counterfactuals require us to clearly identify cause and effect. When we cannot, counterfactual reasoning falls apart.

To demonstrate that an increase in temperature causes an increase in the sales of ice cream and a higher incidence of drowning, we need to prove the counterfactual—that without an increase in temperature, absent some other cause, neither of them would have occurred. In addition, we need to show that there is no causal link between swimmers eating ice cream and drowning.

A connection between the consumption of sweets and drowning is what is known as a confounder, or a link that tricks us into believing that the two are causally related. Other confounders could disprove that temperature is what matters. Perhaps the real cause is that kids are out of school for the summer, with more time for swimming and a greater access to sweet snacks. To prove a counterfactual, we need to correctly identify the causal links between temperature, ice cream sales, the incidence of drowning, and other potential confounders, such as summer vacations, that coincide with a rise in temperature.

Burks was the first researcher to show us how to do this in the social sciences.

Chains, Forks, Colliders, and Confounders

In 1928, Burks coauthored Chapter 2 of the *Yearbook of the National Society for the Study of Education*. This chapter contains the first known causal diagram in the social sciences.[8] It would take another seventy-five years for causal diagrams to become common practice.

Below is the first known causal diagram in the social sciences:[9]

Figure 6.1

BURKS CASUAL DIAGRAM

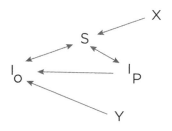

Burks wrote that she was seeking to determine "to what extent are ordinary differences in mental level due to nature and to what extent are they due to nurture?"[10] To answer this question, Burks investigated the causal links between the intelligence of foster children and their parents. *Io* represents the intelligence of the child; *Ip*, the intelligence of the parents; *S*, the cultural status of the family; *Y*, genes not responsible for *Ip* but that contribute to *Io*; and *X*, other unknown factors.

To understand Burks's drawing, some background on causal diagrams is required.

There are three types of causal relationships: chains, forks, and colliders.

Chains are shown in Figure 6.2.

Figure 6.2
___

CHAINS

A ⟶ B ⟶ C

Fire   Smoke   Alarm

Chains are instances in which causality runs from A to B to C. Fire (A) results in smoke (B), which sets off the smoke alarm (C). If we are investigating (C), then we only need to know about (B). We do not need a fire to set off a smoke alarm if something is burning in the oven. Note that in chains, B is called a mediator, standing between A and C; this will be important later to test for causality.

Forks are drawn as shown in Figure 6.3.

Figure 6.3
___

FORKS

B ⟵ A ⟶ C

Ice Cream   Temperature   Drowning

Forks are cases in which A affects both B and C. The relationship between temperature, the consumption of ice cream, and the incidence of drowning is a fork. Higher temperature (A) causes more ice cream to be consumed (B) and more people to jump into the pool (C). Forks are instances in which we can be confused by the odds of two unrelated things occurring at the same time, such as the rates of consumption of ice cream and the incidence of drowning. These two appear to be connected, but that is because they have the same cause: changes in temperature.

Colliders are shown in Figure 6.4.

Figure 6.4

COLLIDERS

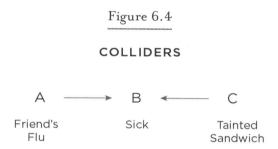

Colliders are examples in which both A and C could affect B. Imagine you have lunch with a friend who is suffering from the flu (A). At lunch, you gobble down a turkey sandwich tainted with salmonella (C). The next day, you feel sick (B). Was it the flu from your friend (A) or the bacteria in the rotten sandwich (C) or both? Colliders can mislead us because an effect could have one or more causes.

Colliders are confounders. As an example, a study published in 1998 by the *New England Journal of Medicine* found that regular walking prolonged life.[11] The researchers followed seven hundred retired men over twelve years and found that the death rate among those who walked more than two miles per day was half that of those who did not. But the researchers correctly identified that men who were younger were both more likely to walk more than two miles per day and live longer.

The causal diagram in Figure 6.5 shows that age is a confounder: it affects both walking and mortality.

Figure 6.5

WALKING AND MORTALITY

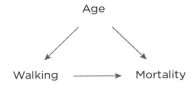

Hence, the researchers in the report added a caveat to their results stating that "the effects on longevity of intentional efforts to increase distance walked per day by physically capable older men cannot be addressed in our study."[12]

Causal diagrams are critical because they show us how to gather counterfactual evidence so we can move beyond association. As we have seen, two variables may be correlated without a causal link between the two, such as the case of ice cream and drowning. Causal diagrams allow us to distinguish between causation and correlation.

Chains and forks both exhibit correlation. But only the former demonstrates causality. In our example of the chain between fire, smoke, and a smoke alarm, there is a correlation between fire and setting off a smoke alarm. There is also a causal relationship between fire and setting off a smoke alarm. In our example of the fork between consumption of ice cream and drowning, there is a correlation between the two. However, there is no causal relationship.

Burks's Study of Intelligence: Nature or Nurture?

In Burks's causal diagram, she explicitly calls out that a child's intelligence is the product of colliders and therefore subject to confounding.

The intelligence of the parents (Ip), the genes not responsible for the intelligence of the parents (Y), and the cultural or social status (S) of the family all impact the intelligence of the child (Io). Burks also states that there is a two-way causal relationship between the intelligence of the child and social status. More intelligent children lead to greater social status, and greater social status offers more opportunities for children to hone their skills. The same two-way causal relationship exists between the intelligence of the parents and social status. Greater intelligence typically improves the social status of an adult, whether in terms of money or recognition. And greater social status raises the perceived intelligence of the parents.

Burks writes:

> *Studies of mental differences among people of different social, educational, or racial groups have sometimes been cited as evidence for the influence of heredity. The position might better be taken that the existence of such differences is simply additional indication of the nature-nurture problem itself.*[13]

Burks is arguing that social status and inherited intelligence are colliders that impact a child's intelligence, and therefore it is difficult to separate out whether either of the two is a causal factor.

In addition, social status is a confounder with regard to a child's inherited mental abilities.

This is the first known scientific study that explicitly calls out and attempts to quantify the confounding effect of social status on intelligence. In her research, Burks was able to identify numerous differences among different classes of children, including the differences in their intelligence quotient measured by standardized tests and the impact of their environment.

Through her collection and parsing of the data, Burks established the importance of a child's environment, including social status. This conclusion was in sharp contrast to the conventional wisdom of the time that differences in IQ were due to genetics. Of course, Burks acknowledged that heredity was an important factor. But she also modeled in her work the two-way relationship between intelligence and social status:

> Let us consider for a moment the correlations of .40 to .50 between the intelligence of siblings or between that of parents and offspring. . . . To what are those due? . . . Children's intelligence may result from differences in cultural status, but those portions contribute to cultural status as well.[14]

Throughout her life, Burks remained an ardent proponent of the belief that environment played a critical role in explaining the educational outcomes between different cohorts of children. And she had the data to prove it, much to the dismay of many.

Burks's data showed the strong influence of the home environment, which could cause a twenty-point increase or decrease in a child's IQ, depending on whether the home environment was favorable or unfavorable.[15]

Burks also was one of the first to question the validity of

standardized intelligence tests, some of which even today remain culturally biased. In 1928, this criticism was unheard of in academic circles.

Burks stated her opinion clearly:

> *The mental ages of children of certain low-testing nationalities commonly turn out to be closer to the norms of American children when measured on non-verbal tests than when measured on verbal ones . . . although both types of tests are called "intelligence" tests, they each measure about as much not held in common as they measure of what is held in common.*[16]

Burks also publicly disagreed with Ronald Fisher's randomization techniques for determining experimental and control groups. Burks warned in a speech that Fisher's method was probably not applicable because it assumes the environment is a random, or chance, factor.[17] But a woman criticizing the leading male statistician of her day did not help her ideas gain traction or improve her standing in the virtually all-male research community.

In another paper, Burks offered the following caution:

> *Making the important assumption that environment works in a random manner . . . Fisher then utilizes the differences actually found between fraternal and parent-child correlations to distinguish between the effects of dominance (e.g., genetics) and those of environment. Consequently, Fisher's method could not be applied to problems of mental heredity without fundamental modifications.*[18]

She admonished future researchers not to rely solely on randomization because researchers should try to actively control the variables in their studies and not passively compile the results.[19] Burks understood, unlike many of her male colleagues, that randomized controlled trials (RCTs) were often not that random. In stark contrast to Fisher, Burks was extremely careful to call out potential confounding influences in her work and clearly identify forks, chains, and colliders.

Three decades later, Fisher and others would not be so meticulous about controlling for confounders in their experiments.

Smoking: It's in Our Genes[20]

On January 11, 1964, the US surgeon general released "Smoking and Health: Report of the Advisory Committee to the Surgeon General of the Public Health Service."[21] This report stated that "cigarette smoking is causally related to lung cancer in men."[22] It was released on a Saturday so as not to disrupt the stock market and was front-page news on every Sunday paper. The advisory committee concluded that smokers on average had a nine- to tenfold risk of developing lung cancer. Until this declaration, and even for years afterward, the claim that smoking caused cancer was hotly contested. Those who doubted that smoking caused lung cancer cited evidence that some smoke their entire lives and are cancer free. And others never smoke but still die from lung cancer.

At the turn of the twentieth century, cigarettes were virtually unknown. It is estimated that 98 percent of tobacco consumption at the time was in the form of chewing products.[23] Eventually, automated manufacturing enabled the mass production of cigarettes. By the 1950s, more than 80 percent of tobacco use was in the form of cigarettes.[24] Not surprisingly, lung cancer was relatively rare during the first half of the twentieth century and then spiked dramatically in the latter half, when it became the leading cause of death among men. Some cited other causes for the rise in lung cancer as confounding factors. A British epidemiologist said in an interview, "Motor cars were a new factor and if I had to put money on anything at the time, I should have put it on motor exhausts or possibly the tarring of roads."[25]

On the side of those claiming that smoking was primarily responsible for the rise in deaths from lung cancer were British researchers Richard Doll and Austin Hill. In 1950, the pair published the article "Smoking and Carcinoma of the Lung" in the September 30 edition of the *British Medical Journal*.[26] They noted that among men in England and Wales the annual number of deaths from lung cancer at twenty leading hospitals rose from 612 to 9,287 from 1922 to 1947, far outstripping the growth in population.[27] Doll and Hill conducted their own study of 2,370 cases of death from lung cancer among men and women and found that nonsmokers were a small fraction of the total. Despite this evidence, the researchers were cautious about immediately reaching the conclusion that smoking causes lung cancer.

Doll and Hill questioned whether the underlying data was truly unbiased and suggested other possible explanations for the patterns in the data: the sample of patients with cancer might not be representative, the control set of patients might not be comparable to the set of patients with cancer, patients might exaggerate their smoking habits, or the interviewers could be biased.[28]

Much of their article discusses these concerns, but ultimately Doll and Hill decided their conclusion was justified. They wrote in summary, "Reasons are given for excluding all these possibilities, and it is concluded that smoking is an important factor in the cause of carcinoma of the lung."[29]

But Doll and Hill had enough concerns about their original study that they subsequently launched what has become known as the British Doctors' Study. Beginning in 1950, the two surveyed sixty thousand British physicians about their smoking habits over the next five years. What they found is that the incidence of lung cancer was twenty-four times higher in smokers compared with nonsmokers.[30]

But some were still not convinced.

On the side of those who doubted that smoking caused cancer was Ronald Fisher.

In 1958, eight years after the publication of the original Doll and Hill paper and three years after confirmation by the British Doctors' Study, Fisher wrote that "unfortunately, considerable propaganda is now being developed to convince the public that cigarette smoking is dangerous."[31] Fisher suggested that, contrary to the research by Doll and Hill, "it would equally be possible to infer . . . that inhaling cigarette smoke was a practice of considerable prophylactic value in preventing the disease."[32] In any case, Fisher said that "to take the poor chap's cigarettes away from him would be rather like taking away his white stick from a blind man. It would make an already unhappy person a little more unhappy than he need be."[33]

One argument Fisher put forward was that smokers might be different, due to a "smoking gene":

> For my part, I think it is more likely that a common cause supplies the explanation. . . . The obvious common cause to think of is the genotype. We are all different genotypes. . . . If there is any genotypic difference between the different smoking classes, we may expect differences in the type or frequency of cancer that they display.[34]

Fisher went on to say that the smoking gene may cause individuals to lead more stressful lives or drink more heavily, and thus suffer a higher incidence of illness. Fisher also speculated that the smoking gene may also cause a person to crave cigarettes.

Subsequent to the Doll and Hill studies, nineteen other studies between 1950 and 1964 reached the same conclusions as Doll and Hill. But Fisher dismissed all of them as unreliable. In his words, these studies were "repetitions of evidence of the same kind, and it is necessary to try to examine whether that kind is sufficient for any scientific conclusion."[35]

While Fisher did not express his opinions in causal diagrams, he was essentially arguing that the smoking gene confounds smoking and lung cancer, as shown in Figure 6.6.

Figure 6.6

FISHER'S SMOKING GENE

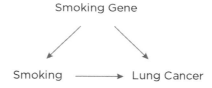

Fisher was adamant that Doll and Hill had not proven that smoking causes cancer because Fisher believed that only RCTs could establish causality. Doll and Hill based their conclusions on an observational study because it was not ethically permissible to conduct an RCT on smoking. An RCT would require randomly assigning two groups of individuals to an experimental group and a control group, in which the former would be forced to smoke.

Fisher wrote:

> *When I spoke to Bradford Hill in the early days of this affair, he was entirely unwilling to claim that causation had been proved . . . Now, randomization is totally impossible, so far as I can judge, in an inquiry of this kind. It is not the fault of the*

*medical investigators. It is not the fault of Hill or
Doll or Hammond that they cannot produce evidence in which a thousand children of teen age
have been laid under a ban that they shall never
smoke, and a thousand more chosen at random
from the same age group have been under compul-
sion to smoke at least thirty cigarettes a day.*[36]

But causal diagrams offer a solution to our inability to
randomize the population of smokers and nonsmokers in an
observational study.

The following diagram was drawn by Judea Pearl, one of the
leading proponents of causal diagrams working today. It demonstrates one approach to test for a causal link between smoking
and lung cancer, given the potential confounding effect of a
smoking gene.[37]

Figure 6.7

PEARL'S SMOKING GENE

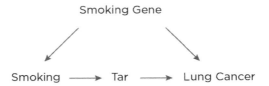

Tar deposits in smokers' lungs are believed to cause cancer. We
can collect data from observational studies on the incidence of tar
in the lungs of smokers and then block the confounding effect of a
smoking gene by controlling for the incidence of tar in the lungs.
Controlling for this variable allows us to factor out the impact of

the smoking gene on mortality caused by smoking; this variable serves as a mediator between smoking and mortality.

By holding smoking constant and varying tar, we can prove there is a causal link between tar and mortality. But we also know there is a causal relationship between smoking and tar. Therefore, we can establish that smoking is tied to mortality, regardless of the confounding effect of a smoking gene. In effect, we are proving the counterfactual: if you do not smoke and have no tar in your lungs, then you will have a lower mortality rate. Our causal diagram shows us how to estimate the probability that a smoker may die from lung cancer using the data from an observational study. With tar as a mediator, we do not need to be concerned about the impact of confounders, such as a smoking gene. All this can be done without conducting an RCT.

The surgeon general's report published in 1964 helped change the minds of many people. By 1968, 78 percent of Americans believed smoking damaged health, up from 48 percent before the report.[38] However, skeptics in the scientific community, led by Fisher and others, continued to put doubt into the minds of many concerning the causal relationship between smoking and lung cancer, even after the report was issued. Throughout his life, Fisher refused to take causal diagrams and nonrandomized experiments seriously. As a result of the scientific controversy surrounding smoking, many lives were unnecessarily lost to lung cancer.

There was a curious aside in the report by the surgeon general's advisory committee. Its scientific panel noted that smoking during pregnancy was beneficial to newborns. This became known as the birth-weight paradox. And it set off another controversy.

Smoking: Better for Babies

In 1959, a study of fifteen thousand children in the San Francisco Bay Area recorded each mother's smoking habits and compared them with the birth weights and mortality rates of newborns.[39] This study noted that although the average weight at birth was seven ounces less for infants of smokers, the mortality rate was significantly lower. The study found that the mortality rates among low-birth-weight babies who had less than thirty-seven weeks of gestation were 336 and 172 per 10,000 for nonsmokers and smokers, respectively.[40] This suggested that smoking was better for babies.

Even back then, few doctors thought smoking by the mother was good for newborns; smoking was known to reduce oxygen transfer across the placenta, and lower birth weights were tied to higher infant mortality. But the data indicated that somehow smoking was connected to a lower rate of neonatal deaths.

The birth-weight paradox remained unsolved for decades until several studies based on causal diagrams uncovered the reason: birth weight was a collider.

Figure 6.8 shows the causal diagram for the birth-weight paradox.

Figure 6.8
_____

BIRTH WEIGHT PARADOX

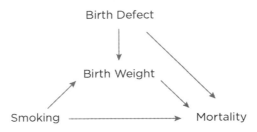

As we can see, birth weight is a collider that is negatively affected by smoking and birth defects. If the mother was a smoker, that explained why a baby was underweight. If the mother was not a smoker, an underweight baby likely suffered from a birth defect.

Hence, low-weight babies of nonsmokers typically have birth defects, whereas low-weight babies of smokers generally do not. That is why the low-weight babies of nonsmokers have a higher mortality rate than the low-weight babies of smokers. As a collider, birth weight confounds what we are trying to measure—newborn mortality.

Another example of the impact of confounders is racial bias in law enforcement.

Racial Bias in Policing: Unstopped Whites

Racial bias in policing has been widely reported on in recent years. Numerous studies have been conducted that analyze a range of outcomes, including the use of force by police officers. However, many of these studies suffer from the confounding effects of the records themselves: the evidence of racial bias in policing is based on evidence collected by the police, and that evidence itself may be the product of racial bias.

Researchers from Princeton University employed causal diagrams to untangle the racial bias behind police records.[41] Specifically, they looked at whether there is racial bias in the decision to stop a suspected criminal. This is important because police records are based on interactions with those who are stopped; instances in which individuals are not stopped are not part of police records. But this could lead to misrepresenting racial bias in policing.

A common proxy for racial bias in policing is the relative proportion of police-civilian encounters with white people and people of color that lead to a use of force. If a higher portion of such encounters with people of color results in the use of force, then that could be evidence for racial bias in policing.

To illustrate the potential confounding effect of racial bias in police records, assume that white people are stopped only when police witness the commission of a crime and people of color are stopped all the time. The portion of stops that lead to a use of force against white people will be higher than that for people of color, as most of the stops of people of color will be ordinary citizens going about their daily lives. Given these assumptions, the data should show a bias against white people in policing, as encounters with white people are more likely to lead to police violence.

In fact, this apparent bias against white people is just the confounding effect of racial bias that is rooted in the initial decision of whom to stop. In this example, the exclusion of many unstopped white people from our sample misleads us into believing there is a bias against white people in policing.

The Princeton researchers identified this confounding effect with the following causal diagram.[42]

Figure 6.9

RACIAL BIAS IN POLICING

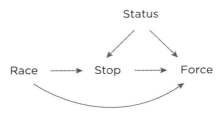

Status affects whether a person is stopped and whether the use of force occurs. Status is assumed to include a host of other characteristics, such as past criminal record, social status, and neighborhood. Race also affects whether a person is stopped and whether force is used. Race is separate from status as it relates only to skin color in this study.

As this causal diagram makes clear, status and race are confounding effects on whether a person is stopped and whether force is used. Hence, we cannot reach valid inferences about racial bias in policing without adjusting for the confounding effect of both in the underlying police records. This requires testing two counterfactuals: one for white people and another for people of color. For white people, we would like to know what would have happened if they had been stopped but were not because of racial bias. For people of color, we want to determine what portion would not have been stopped if they had been a white person.

With the benefit of causal diagrams, the Princeton researchers reevaluated the conclusions from a previous study based on the use of force against white people and people of color from the New York Police Department's Stop, Question, and Frisk database of roughly five million pedestrian stops from 2003 to 2013.[43] The data showed, as expected, that the threshold of observed criminal activity required to trigger stops of white people was higher than that of people of color. The police in New York City stopped white people and people of color who were committing crimes, but they also stopped a lot of people of color who were not. Given that more of the white people stopped by police were committing crimes, the researchers should have found a bias against white people in policing, because on a percentage basis encounters between white people and police should more frequently lead to a use of force. But the data showed that encounters with people of color were more likely to result in the use of force by police.

This demonstrated the underlying bias in police records, due to the omission of many "unstopped whites." Moreover, the large number of unstopped white people was more than offset by a greater use of force against people of color. Hence, researchers showed that racial bias in policing was greater than anyone had suspected. They concluded that "the conventional approach underestimates discriminatory force by a factor of at least four."[44] In terms of numbers, the authors of the study estimated that over that ten-year period in New York City, "there were 75,000 instances in which police laid hands on black and Hispanic civilians but would not have done so had those individuals been white."[45]

The Princeton researchers went on to emphasize the importance of collecting data on race as it relates to the first stages of encounters between police and civilians. Without this information, any efforts at reforming police practices may be misguided or ineffective.[46]

Conclusions

Correlation is not causation. To show correlation, we only need to show that A is regularly associated with B. To prove causation, we also need to prove the counterfactual: A is sufficient but not necessary to result in B.

Causal diagrams help us prove counterfactuals by providing a method to identify confounded and unconfounded causal links. Causal diagrams enable us to analyze the effect of walking on mortality and social status on a child's intelligence, the relationships between smoking and lung cancer and birth weight, and the severity of racial bias in policing. Importantly, causal diagrams allow us to go beyond RCTs and draw conclusions from observational studies. In many instances, RCTs, such as in the case of smoking and lung cancer, may not be feasible or ethical.

In the final chapter, we will apply causal diagrams and Bayes' theorem, two of the most powerful tools in the social sciences, to the politics of COVID-19. We will see that the poisoned politics surrounding this disease that has plagued America has at its root "alternative facts."

CHAPTER 7

COVID-19: Misinformation and My Tribe

Alternative Facts: COVID-19 and an Election

The COVID-19 pandemic has widened the political divide in the United States. In a 2020 poll, 77 percent of Americans believed the discord between Republicans and Democrats was greater than it was at the time of the initial outbreak.[1] At the close of 2021, an estimated 90 percent of Democrats had been vaccinated compared with 58 percent of Republicans.[2] Most Democrats report they have or will get a booster, while most Republicans say they will not.[3] While 64 percent of Democrats were worried about contracting COVID-19, only about one-third of Republicans had the same fears.[4] In the same survey, 63 percent of Democrats and only 29 percent of Republicans thought that people in their community should regularly wear a mask. Many Republicans were particularly incensed by mask mandates. One woman wrote, "We all learned in Microbiology 101 that [masks] don't work . . . I am disgusted with people who wear masks."[5] A man stated, "I refused lockdown, I refuse masks, I refuse to participate in any of this bogus crap."[6]

The stark contrasts in views on COVID-19 are just one example of a growing schism along political and cultural lines. A Pew Research Center poll showed that the political polarization between Republicans and Democrats doubled between 1978 and 2019.[7] Over the period from 1960 to 2008, Americans were twice as likely to think members of the other party were more selfish than they were and eight times more likely to believe members of the opposing party were less intelligent.[8] In 1960, 5 percent of Americans reported they would be upset if their child married someone from the other political party. By 2010, that number was more than 40 percent.[9] It is no longer just business: it is personal.

Of course, there have been periods in our history when Americans were even more at odds with each other. In the late eighteenth century, there was armed conflict between those who favored independence from Great Britain and Royalists who wished to remain part of the British Empire. There was a wide political and cultural chasm between Democrats in the South and Republicans in the North in the decades leading up to and following the Civil War. During these periods of American history, the political and cultural gulf between partisans was even greater than that which exists today between urban Democrats and rural Republicans. Nevertheless, while not comparable to the most divisive periods in our nation's history, the split between liberals and conservatives has widened over the past decades.

In my view, what distinguishes today's political strife from that of the past is that our disagreements are not only over ideology but also over facts.

The data concerning mask wearing and the risks of an individual contracting COVID-19 are a matter of science—not ideology. So, too, are some basic economic and political realities. Republicans are twice as likely as Democrats to think the average immigrant receives more government transfer payments than a longtime US resident.[10] And 78 percent of Democrats but only 61 percent of Republicans believe income inequality has increased over the past decade.[11] Among Republicans, 55 percent agree with the statement that the US Capitol riot on January 6, 2021, was "led by violent left-wing protestors trying to make Trump look bad."[12] And 76 percent of Republicans believe that Donald Trump received more votes in the 2020 presidential election than Joe Biden.[13]

One political commentator called these disagreements "the polarization of reality."[14] It is understandable that partisans will disagree when it comes to ideology. But facts?

Fighting the Infection of Alternative Facts

As discussed in Chapter 4, Bayes' theorem provides a quantitative method to update our beliefs based on new information. As we have seen, it is a powerful tool that has proven effective in a variety of uses, from locating submarines resting deep below the ocean waves to blocking unwanted emails detailing the benefits of Viagra.

By employing Bayes' theorem, Democrats and Republicans should be able to reach a consensus on basic facts. Two individuals may start with opposing beliefs. For example, partisans may initially hold widely divergent views on the effectiveness of wearing masks to slow the spread of COVID-19. However, as evidence from observational studies comes forward, individuals from opposite ends of the political spectrum should revise their respective beliefs and eventually reach common ground. Similarly, partisans may initially disagree about the extent of social and economic mobility and income inequality or the amount of transfer payments received by immigrants. Or they may disagree on who received more votes in the 2020 presidential election. But it should be just a matter of time until enough evidence is presented for Democrats and Republicans to agree on who is the legitimate forty-sixth president of the United States. In theory, if Bayes' theorem is applied correctly, a broad consensus should eventually emerge on basic facts.

Figure 7.1 is a causal diagram that lays out how Bayes' theorem should enable individuals to reach a consensus.

Figure 7.1

BAYES' THEOREM

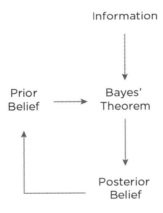

A piece of information and a prior belief about the likelihood something is true are fed into Bayes' theorem. Based on the information, we estimate a new posterior belief. This revised belief becomes the new prior with which to evaluate additional information. Just as in the case of tossing balls on a square table or estimating the probability that a coin is fair, we arrive at a more accurate belief with each new piece of information. Given enough additional information, partisans should eventually converge on a consensus about basic facts, regardless of how disparate their initial prior beliefs were.

In the case of COVID-19, if scientific studies conclude that masks are effective, then the views of Democrats and Republicans should come together over time, as the members of each party revise their prior beliefs to reflect the mounting evidence of mask efficacy. Alternatively, studies may emerge demonstrating that donning a mask is largely ineffective. In this instance, the members of both parties should revise their respective beliefs about the efficacy of masks downward. In either case, Democrats and Republicans should, in theory, eventually agree on basic facts—either wearing masks is effective or it is not—based on the application of Bayes' theorem to each new piece of evidence. Bayes' theorem provides a means for even those at opposite ends of the political spectrum to agree on basic facts, given sufficient time and evidence.

Let's illustrate the use of Bayes' theorem to reach consensus with a specific example involving the effectiveness of masks to slow the spread of COVID-19.

Bayes, Masks, and the Political Divide

Suppose that 80 percent of Democrats and 20 percent of Republicans start with an initial belief that masks are effective in slowing the spread of COVID-19. A new study is published concluding that masks are effective. Both Democrats and Republicans believe that the probability the new study is valid is 60 percent.

We can think about this in terms of the COVID-19 test in Chapter 4. In that example, the COVID-19 test was 90 percent accurate. Given 90 percent accuracy, we were able to calculate the chances that you actually were sick, measured by the ratio of true positives to the sum of true and false positives. If partisans believe the new study is 60 percent accurate, this is comparable to a COVID-19 test that is 60 percent accurate. True positive evidence that masks are effective is then the equivalent of a true positive COVID-19 test result. False positive evidence that masks work is like a false positive COVID-19 test result, and so on. The percentage of those who believe masks are effective will be the ratio of those who believe the new study provides true positive evidence divided by the sum of those who believe the new study provides true positive evidence and those who discount the new study because they think it contains false positive evidence.

Let's start from the perspective of Democrats.

Figure 7.2

DEMOCRATS AND COVID

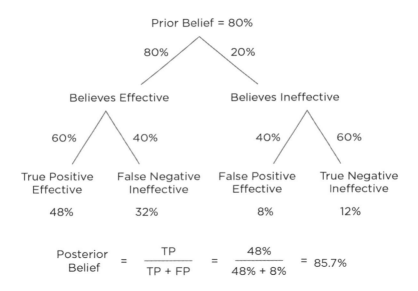

Prior Belief = 80%

80% / \ 20%

Believes Effective   Believes Ineffective

60% / \ 40%   40% / \ 60%

True Positive   False Negative   False Positive   True Negative
Effective   Ineffective   Effective   Ineffective

48%   32%   8%   12%

$$\text{Posterior Belief} = \frac{TP}{TP + FP} = \frac{48\%}{48\% + 8\%} = 85.7\%$$

Among Democrats, initially 80 percent believe masks are effective, and 20 percent are convinced they are not. The new study concluding that masks are effective reinforces the existing views of 80 percent of Democrats and conflicts with the opinions of the remaining 20 percent. All Democrats (those who believe masks are effective and those who believe masks are ineffective) view the study as 60 percent reliable.

Among those who view masks as effective, the new study provides 48 percent true positive evidence confirming their initial beliefs. For those who view masks as ineffective, the new study contains 8 percent false positive evidence that masks are ineffective. The ratio of true positives to the sum of true positives and false positives is (48%/(48% + 8%)) or 85.7 percent. In other words, if you ask all Democrats, based on the new study, whether mask wearing is effective, then 85.7 percent will answer yes, a higher percentage than the original 80 percent of Democrats who believed in the efficacy of masks.

This makes sense. The study is a new piece of evidence that indicates masks are effective, and it is believed to be 60 percent reliable. We would therefore expect the percentage of Democrats who believe that masks are effective to increase.

Next, let's consider the perspective of Republicans.

Figure 7.3

REPUBLICANS AND COVID

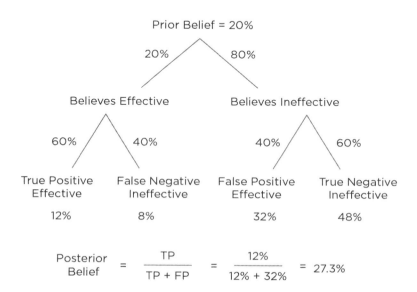

Among Republicans, initially 20 percent believe masks are effective, and 80 percent are convinced they are not. The new study concluding that masks are effective reinforces the existing views of 20 percent of Republicans and conflicts with the opinions of the remaining 80 percent. All Republicans (those who believe masks are effective and those who believe masks are ineffective) view the study as 60 percent accurate.

Among those who view masks as effective, the new study provides 12 percent true positive evidence confirming their initial beliefs. For those who view masks as ineffective, the new study contains 32 percent false positive evidence that masks are effective. The ratio of true positives to the sum of true positives and false positives is (12%/(12% + 32%)) or 27.3 percent. In other words, if you ask all Republicans, based on the new study, whether mask wearing is effective, then 27.3 percent will answer yes, a higher percentage than the original 20 percent of Republicans who believed in the efficacy of masks.

This also makes sense. The new study should increase the percent of Republicans who believe that masks are effective, just as it did for the Democrats.

After publication of the new study, partisans of both parties should have greater confidence in the efficacy of masks. If additional evidence continues to come forward concluding that masks are effective, then Democrats and Republicans should eventually reach a consensus, despite their initial disparate beliefs, that masks limit the spread of COVID-19.

But a basic fact that we can all agree on is that despite two years and hundreds of scientific studies, Democrats and Republicans do not agree on the effectiveness of masks.

In my view, this is due to misinformation and its impact on our reasoning.

We Are Not Immune to the Disease of Misinformation

The causal diagram in Figure 7.1 assumes the evidence presented is unbiased. But if some or most of the new evidence is misinformation, then Bayes' theorem may not yield more accurate answers. Reasoning based on false premises can yield invalid conclusions. Thus, we need to filter out misinformation as an input to Bayes' theorem.

But on what basis do we decide what is misinformation?

In an ideal world, we would conduct extensive research on a piece of new evidence to determine its validity. However, that often involves significant time and effort. So, most individuals filter out misinformation by discounting the odds that the new evidence is true—and they do this based on their prior beliefs. Partisans may label what they suspect to be misinformation as either "alternative facts" or "fake news."

Returning to the example of David Hume and Richard Price, a committed theist will be inclined to take the report of a miracle in a country halfway around the world at face value. On the other hand, an equally committed atheist will be highly skeptical of the circumstances surrounding an apparently unexplainable occurrence that violates the laws of nature. Both the theist and atheist could leave their work and family and travel halfway around the globe and spend weeks conducting an extensive investigation to determine whether the reported miracle really happened. But the more likely case is that neither will immediately book a flight upon news of the reported miracle. Instead, the conclusions reached by the theist and atheist concerning the likelihood that a miracle occurred will be based on their prior beliefs. This is not irrational: the benefit gained by knowing whether the reported miracle actually occurred does not justify the costs of determining whether it did.

Therefore, we should add a filter to our causal diagram that models Bayesian reasoning; the filter should reflect the way we discount the validity of new information based on our prior beliefs.

Figure 7.4

BAYES' THEOREM AND MISINFORMATION

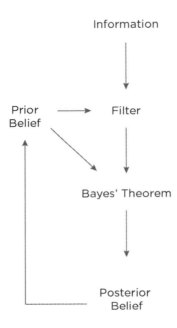

As before, we begin with a piece of information and a prior belief. Next, we apply a filter based on our prior belief to determine the likely accuracy of the information. In our example of Hume and Price, theists will be highly confident that the new evidence is not misinformation. By contrast, atheists will be equally as confident that the new evidence is misinformation and ignore it. Agnostics will judge the probability that the evidence of a miracle is true as somewhere between these two extremes.

Hence, there is a causal relationship between prior beliefs, filters for misinformation, and Bayesian reasoning. Prior briefs are confounders, as they affect the estimation of posterior beliefs through Bayesian reasoning and filters for misinformation. This is not surprising. Most people give more credence to evidence that is consistent with their prior beliefs.

To illustrate the effect of misinformation and filters on Bayesian reasoning, let's reconsider the example laid out in Figure 7.3 about the effectiveness of masks from the perspective of Republicans.

Suppose that Republicans believe the evidence from the study may be misinformation. Republicans do not completely discount the study but are more skeptical than Democrats, because the study's conclusion that masks are effective challenges their prior belief. Assume that Republicans therefore lower the probability that the new study is accurate from 60 percent to 40 percent.

Republicans would then reestimate their initial beliefs as shown in Figure 7.5.

Figure 7.5

REPUBLICANS, COVID, AND MISINFORMATION

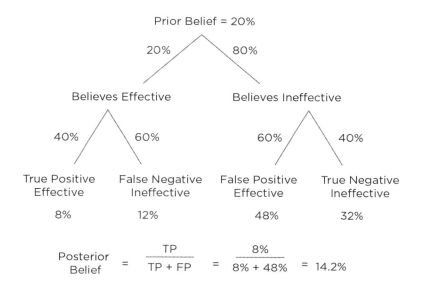

Among those who view masks as effective, the study provides 8 percent true positive evidence confirming their initial beliefs. For those who view masks as ineffective, the study contains 48 percent false positive evidence that masks are effective. The ratio of true positives to the sum of true positives and false positives is (8%/(8% + 48%)) or 14.2 percent. In other words, if you ask all Republicans, based on the study, whether mask wearing is effective, then 14.2 percent will answer yes, a lower percentage than the original 20 percent of Republicans who believed in the efficacy of masks.

Notice what has happened. The initial divergence in beliefs between Democrats and Republicans was 60 percent (80% – 20%). After the study that concluded that wearing masks is effective was published, the partisan gap widened to 71.5 percent (85.7% – 14.2%). The net effect of the publication of a study indicating masks are effective is a further polarization of views on the effectiveness of wearing a mask. Even though Democrats and Republicans were presented with the same piece of new information, the disagreement over basic facts between the two sides grew.

Confirmation Bias: A Not-Irrational Choice

In a world with misinformation, we often filter new evidence through prior beliefs. Some have labeled the viewing of new evidence through the lens of prior belief as "confirmation" or "myside" bias.[15] This bias is generally viewed as irrational, something that should be avoided. But given that determining the accuracy of a new piece of information is frequently costly, it is reasonable to base our view of that new information partly on prior beliefs. This is particularly true because we are often not subject matter experts and thus have to rely on the opinions of those who are.

In our everyday lives, determining the validity of a new piece of information is often a function of our prior beliefs about the competence and trustworthiness of the source. We trust our doctor when he tells us the heart in our chest is beating irregularly or our auto mechanic when she states that the engine in our car is misfiring. Alternatively, we could quit our current job and enroll in a medical or automotive repair school and after graduation decide for ourselves. But the costs of switching professions would be prohibitively expensive in time, money, and effort. So, we form a judgment, based on prior beliefs, concerning the expertise of those we rely on to take care of our bodies and cars.[16]

But it is not enough just to believe an expert is qualified to render an opinion. We also need to be convinced that those we rely on have our best interests in mind. If we believe that the recommendation for a new heart or new engine is driven solely by pecuniary motives, then we will seek out another medical or automotive professional. We need to determine whether these professionals are trustworthy before proceeding with a risky heart surgery or an expensive auto repair.

In my view, most instances of what some have labeled confirmation bias are not irrational. Rather, they simply reflect the fact that relying on experts, whom we believe to be competent and trustworthy, is cost effective and, in some cases, the only practical alternative. (We might be able to swap out an engine in our automobile, but the same is not true for the heart in our chest.) Our prior opinions on the competency and trustworthiness of those experts are not an irrational basis for filtering out misinformation, whether it is the longevity of the heart under our ribs or the remaining hours on the engine under the hood of our car.

In addition, if confirmation bias is fundamentally irrational, then there would be a negative correlation between cognitive ability and the incidence of this bias. Studies have shown that a long list of biases, such as anchoring, hindsight, the gambler's fallacy, base rate, and sample size, have a statistically significant negative correlation with CART, a test that assesses levels of ratio-nal thinking.[17] These studies have demonstrated that those who score highly on CART are largely immune from the biases listed previously.[18] However, there is no correlation between the ability to score highly on CART and confirmation bias.[19] (Confirmation bias is also nonpartisan: Republicans and Democrats are equally vulnerable to this alleged defect in reasoning.[20]) If confirmation bias is a cognitive defect, then those with greater cognitive abili-ties would suffer less from this example of flawed reasoning, like other types of biases. They do not. Either confirmation bias is fundamentally different from any other human bias, or it is not a bias at all.

This reliance on prior beliefs becomes even more important in a world filled with misinformation. The greater the amount of misinformation, the more we must rely on prior beliefs. The more we filter out information that disagrees with our prior beliefs, the more likely it is that new information will reinforce our prior beliefs. In our example, Republicans lowered their estimate of the reliability of the study that concluded masks are effective to 40 percent, as only 20 percent of fellow Republicans believed masks were effective. This lowered the percentage of Republicans who, based on the study, believed masks are effective to 14.2 percent. At the same time, Democrats viewed the new piece of evidence as confirmatory and raised their estimation that masks are effective to 85.7 percent.

Hence, we have become trapped in a vicious circle of misin-formation and distrust that reinforces prior beliefs and further divides Democrats and Republicans. Our dependency on prior beliefs has only increased with the proliferation of misinforma-tion and an increase in our unwillingness to trust those with whom we disagree.

This is particularly true when it comes to news.

The Media Divide: Broadcasting to Narrowcasting

For decades after World War II, most Americans got their news from local newspapers and one of three television networks (ABC, CBS, or NBC) in the form of a suppertime broadcast. Network anchors, such as Walter Cronkite or David Brinkley, strove to provide unbiased reporting. Local newspapers and network news both claimed to present unbiased information. Pool reporters for the Associated Press, Reuters, and other organizations whose articles were distributed to newspapers across the nation aimed to supply nonpartisan stories. Whether the source was a television broadcast or a newspaper, there was a broad consensus in the media and among the American public about basic facts.

But that consensus has been shattered.

One of the primary causes of the weakening of a national consensus about basic facts is the decline in the viewership of network news. Back in the 1950s, most American families regularly gathered in the early evening around the new device in the living room called the television. Together, they watched trusted anchors and television journalists stationed around the world report on the day's events. Today, less than 40 percent of Americans regularly get news from television.[21] And those who do get their news from television are older: 68 percent of those over sixty-five regularly watch television news compared with 16 percent of those aged eighteen to twenty-nine.[22]

In addition, television news has become more partisan. In 1996, MSNBC and Fox News were founded. The executives at the cable news networks realized that many viewers preferred echo chambers to public squares. The economics of cable news is also compelling: it is much cheaper to pay a talking head to spout their opinions than to pay the salaries of hundreds of journalists around the world to undertake extensive investigative reporting.

This trend was exacerbated by the demise of newspapers. In

1950, the paid daily circulation for US newspapers was fifty-three million, or 1.2 newspapers per household.[23] By 2010, daily paid circulation was forty-three million, or 0.3 newspapers per household.[24] Today, newspapers are a primary source of news for less than 10 percent of the American public.[25]

In contrast to that world of the 1950s, 86 percent of Americans report regularly using a smartphone, tablet, or computer to find news on social media, search engines, and websites. Newspapers and television are no longer the primary source of news for most Americans. Unfortunately, the online delivery of news is plagued with filter bubbles, some created by the technology companies and some of our own making. Facebook and Google employ algorithms that limit exposure to information that conflicts with a user's worldview and instead promote stories and websites that are politically congenial. The use of these algorithms by the leading tech companies is not an effort to sway public opinion but simply a way to make more money: these companies have learned that users will engage more often with content that reinforces and does not challenge prior beliefs.

The users of these platforms (that's us) are also to blame. Most of us segregate ourselves into like-minded online communities: the median share of friends who are ideologically aligned within the average Facebook network exceeds 80 percent.[26] We further compound the media political divide by mostly sharing stories that are consistent with the political bias of the recipients. In turn, the recipients share those stories with other like-minded individuals. Within an online group with homogenous political views, studies have shown that even factually incorrect stories can go viral, as misinformation rarely falls into the hands of those who question its validity.[27]

One study reached the following conclusion:

Users tend to aggregate in communities of interest, which causes reinforcement and fosters confirmation, segregation, and polarization. This comes at the expense of the quality of the information and leads to proliferation of biased narratives fomented by unsubstantiated rumors, mistrust, and paranoia.[28]

This is not to claim that the average consumer of online news of either political party is being duped. Most Americans believe that the news they receive over the internet is largely inaccurate.[29] This mistrust also extends to other media. The percentage of people who believe that major news outlets can be relied on to be fair and honest has shrunk from 72 percent in 1976 to 32 percent today.[30] But this only reinforces a reliance on prior beliefs, as a rising percentage of the news we receive is perceived to be misinformation.

Over the past decades, the media industry has transitioned from broadcasting (network news and newspapers) to narrowcasting (cable news and online). This has contributed to the mistrust Americans now feel toward the sources of much of their information.

The Physical Divide: Priuses and Pickups

Just as in the digital world, Americans have been steadily forming like-minded communities in the physical world. By primarily interacting with other individuals with the same views in our neighborhoods and places of work, we effectively filter out information that challenges our prior beliefs, whether intentionally or unintentionally.

The largest, most heavily Democratic states are in the Northeast and on the West Coast. The South remains overwhelmingly Republican, as many white Southerners switched to the Republican Party during the 1960s due to the passage of civil rights legislation by a Democratic president. With the exception of a few large urban areas, most Southerners remain faithful to the GOP to the present day. In 2016, Hillary Clinton lost all of the Southern states and almost all of the interior states while sweeping the Northeastern states and West Coast. In 2020, Biden was able—by the thinnest of margins—to turn several previously red states blue, but many analysts believe that without the COVID-19 pandemic Trump would have won those states and the presidency.

In fact, population density is an even more reliable indicator of party allegiance. The median population density for the average Democrat is 1,197 people per square mile compared with 585 for the average Republican.[31] Counties with more than eight hundred people per square mile are almost always Democratic, and those less densely populated are mostly Republican.[32] In 2016, Trump garnered a greater number of votes than Clinton in 2,584 of the nation's 3,056 counties.[33] But the counties Trump won represented only 45% of the nation's population.[34] It was Clinton's overwhelming wins in many of the nation's most populous counties that earned her more popular votes. In 2020, Trump won 2,547 counties compared to 509 for Biden.[35] Biden won the presidency based on the urban vote.

Over the last several decades, the political divide between urban and rural counties has grown. More Americans than ever are living in what analysts call "landslide counties," defined as those in which the winning presidential candidate received more than 60 percent of the vote. In 1992, 39 percent of voters lived in landslide counties.[36] By 2016, that number was 61 percent.[37]

Post-Truth: The Word of the Year

In 2016, the *Oxford English Dictionary* (OED) named "post-truth" the word of the year. This was after a more than 2,000 percent spike in the word's appearance during 2015.[38] According to the OED, post-truth is "an adjective defined as relating or denoting circumstances in which objective facts are less influential in shaping public opinion than appeals to emotions and personal belief."[39]

Today, we live in a post-truth world in which there is no longer a broad consensus on many matters of fact. The amount of misinformation in our world is greater than ever and so, too, our reliance on prior belief. We are less challenged in our beliefs than ever before because Democrats and Republicans are increasingly separated in the online and off-line worlds, as partisans silo themselves in opposing virtual and geographical communities. But associating with like-minded individuals hinders us from challenging prior beliefs.

America as a nation is becoming more diverse. Yet, our virtual worlds and neighborhoods are becoming more homogenous. The emergence of landslide communities, online and off-line, is worsening the "polarization of facts."

The rise of more landslide communities also compounds the asymmetry between the benefits of supporting a candidate you like compared with the costs of offending those who like you. The upside of voting for the candidate you favor is theoretical. The odds that one ballot will determine the result of any election involving thousands or millions of voters are infinitesimal. On the other hand, the downside of supporting a candidate your community opposes is real. You risk suffering the disdain of friends, neighbors, and coworkers. Of course, you can publicly back one candidate and privately vote for another. But most voters find such duplicity impractical and uncomfortable and pick a political horse to ride.

Unfortunately, the less politically diverse a community, the more opprobrium a person is likely to suffer from supporting a candidate opposed by others. A community in which all but a few champion the same candidate is less likely to tolerate a diversity of political views. A community in which each person backs a different candidate is more likely to allow for dissenting opinions. The more politically rigid an in-person or online community, the more pushback you get for supporting the other side.

From the perspective of an individual voter, it may be the rational choice to ignore basic facts to justify support of a candidate your community idolizes. My support of a particular candidate will not determine whether they are elected. But it may decide whether I am invited to next Sunday's picnic. Or get publicly flamed on social media.

It's my vote versus my tribe.

Conclusions

A meta-analysis of studies sampling the views of Democrats and Republicans showed that partisans from both parties on average were equally biased in favor of their respective camps.[40] One example is how they regard the effectiveness of masks in preventing the spread of COVID-19. As opinions on mask efficacy have become polarized, partisans have become less inclined to view new studies concerning mask efficacy with an unbiased eye.

On April 23, 2020, during a White House press conference, then-President Trump suggested injecting chemical cleaners into the bloodstream or lungs to treat COVID-19:

> *I see the disinfectant where it knocks it out in a minute. One minute. And is there a way we can do something like that, by injection inside or almost a cleaning. Because you see it gets in the lungs, and it does a tremendous number on the lungs.*[41]

Trump's approval ratings among Republicans and Democrats in the week following his remarks did not change.[42] This new piece of evidence concerning the thought process of the then-president during a time of national crisis did not change the prior beliefs of Democrats and Republicans one iota. At the time, every Republican I know stated that Trump was joking, and every Democrat I spoke with swore he was serious. While not a scientific poll with a statistically significant sample size, my survey does illustrate that our view of the world depends on where we stand.

The post-truth world in which we live is partly due to the proliferation of misinformation, which causes us to rely on prior beliefs. It is also partly due to Americans sorting themselves into more homogenous communities online and in person. Echo chambers within our computers, tablets, and phones are bad enough. Now, diverse voices are less frequently heard within our neighborhoods as the nation divides itself between urban Democrats and rural Republicans. This is compounded by the asymmetry between the benefits of supporting the candidate you like and the costs of opposing the candidate of those who like you. The combination of the preceding leads voters to adopt increasingly extreme political views and to disagree on basic facts, such as the effectiveness of masks (and disinfectant) to combat COVID-19.

Some have argued that the splintering of the mainstream media and sorting of Democrats and Republicans into urban and rural communities are just symptoms of a more fundamental underlying disease—a gaping political divide in the country. Some argue that the media is simply giving partisans what they want and that like-minded individuals are congregating precisely because the country is becoming more diverse.

In my judgment, causality runs in both directions. America does suffer from a widening political gulf that the media exploits. The response by some people to greater diversity has been to move. But the splintering of the media and the sorting of Democrats and Republicans into separate communities will only serve to further divide an already divided nation.

Epilogue

WE HAVE SEEN HOW PROBABILITY misleads us.

Hundreds of thousands of years of *Homo sapiens* evolution have not prepared us to compute the odds for simple games with dice or game shows with goats. We are confused by the odds when rendering a verdict on the guilt of an ex-football star, insulating our investments from the next stock market (or bitcoin) crash, or evaluating the efficacy of a new drug based on a randomized controlled trial.

We can state many things with confidence. It is highly probable that if we drop a pencil it will fall to the floor, just like it did yesterday. We can assign an equally high probability to the outcome of computing the area of a right triangle—the correct answer will be the product of the two sides divided by two, as it has been for more than two thousand years. Fortunately, throughout human history, the laws of nature and the first principles of mathematics have not changed. At least not yet.

However, all human reasoning is still based on induction. Our estimate of the likelihood that A caused B is based on past experience, and future results may vary. To varying degrees, our understanding of the past and predictions about the future have a degree of uncertainty and therefore are subject to the laws of probability. In addition, our brains and the symbols contained within them have been shaped by evolution to produce more babies, not to accurately represent the world around us. Our reasoning evolved for survival in prehistoric times, not to thrive in the modern world. This includes evaluating the chances we are infected with COVID-19 based on a positive test result.

Thankfully, we have two powerful tools to help us deal with uncertainty and the limitations of brains shaped by evolution: Bayes' theorem and causal diagrams. Bayes' theorem enables us to revise our initial beliefs based on new evidence. Causal diagrams allow us to separate causation from correlation.

Today, the limits of human reasoning are apparent, as we disagree over basic facts, including the dangers of COVID-19 and the results of an election. It is more important than ever not to be confused by the odds.

Acknowledgments

I AM FORTUNATE ONCE AGAIN to have Stewart Ethier partner with me on this book. He much improved the original manuscript, correcting numerous technical and not-so-technical errors. He was particularly helpful in the construction of the decision trees presented in Chapters 4 and 7. Stewart has a true gift of explaining the complex in intuitive terms. His students were lucky to have him as a professor.

Gary Williams once again played an important role in the conception, covers, and content of the work. His encouragement to keep at it made all the difference. A former Goldman Sachs coworker, Emanual Derman, critiqued Chapter 2, which is partly based on what I learned from him years ago. "Eman" is one of few individuals who has reached the top of his profession in academics and on the trading floors of Wall Street. It was a pleasure to work with him then and now. I also owe a debt to another Goldman Sachs colleague, Fischer Black, and my co-lecturer at Stanford, Myron Scholes, whose work inspired many of the ideas in this book.

The team at Greenleaf came through once gain. This is my third book with Justin Branch, Tyler LeBleu, and Chase Quarterman, and they again surpassed high expectations. Sally Garland is one of the best senior editors in the business and excelled for a third time, particularly at those pesky permissions. Judy Marchman copyedited once again with her exceptionally perceptive sharp eye, and Tonya

Trybula proofread the final manuscript with pinpoint precision. I have described Heather Settler as a collaborator as much as a developmental editor and that remains true. As usual, Heather forced me to delete and clarify parts of the original longer, muddled manuscript. The end product is a crisper and clearer book.

To my family, your love and support during the past two COVID years means the world to me. We spent a lot more days together at home—which was a really good thing for me. As I write this, we are getting back to normal, at least for now. I hope the new normal includes the same amount of family time.

This book is dedicated to you.

References

Acemoglu, Daron, Asuman Ozdaglar, and James Siderius. 2022. "A Model of Online Misinformation." NBER Working Paper Series, No. 28884. Revised January 2022. https://www.nber.org/system/files/working_papers/w28884/w28884.pdf.

Adler, Jerry. 2017. "The Reformation: Can Social Scientists Save Themselves?: An Intellectual Crisis in the Age of TED Talks and Freakonomics." *Pacific Standard*. Updated June 14, 2017. https://psmag.com/social-justice/can-social-scientists-save-themselves-human-behavior-78858#.k02xjt1hw.

Aldrich, John. 2008. "R. A. Fisher on Bayes and Bayes' Theorem." *Bayesian Analysis* 3, No. 1, 161–170.

Alesina, Alberto, Armando Miano, and Stefanie Stantcheva. 2020. "The Polarization of Reality." AEA Papers and Proceedings 2020, 110, 324–328. https://scholar.harvard.edu/files/stantcheva/files/polarization_reality.pdf.

Allen, Arthur. 2007. *Vaccine: The Controversial Story of Medicine's Greatest Lifesaver*. New York: W.W. Norton.

Allred, Kristen. 2018. "The Causes and Effects of 'Filter Bubbles' and how to Break Free." Medium.com. April 13, 2018. https://medium.com/@10797952/the-causes-and-effects-of-filter-bubbles-and-how-to-break-free-df6c5cbf919f.

Al-Shawaf, Laith. 2020. "Optimism and the Inquisition: The Extraordinary Life of Girolamo Cardano." PopMatters. March 3, 2020. https://www.popmatters.com/girolamo-cardano-scholarship-and-tragedy-2645368482.html.

Arkin, Marc M. 1995. "'The Intractable Principle:' David Hume, James Madison, Religion, and the Tenth Federalist." *The American Journal of Legal History* 39, no. 2 (April 1995), 148–176. https://www.jstor.org/stable/845899?read-now=1&refreqid=excelsior%3A6ef03fe90d9df2efee1d12ee7bfff07d&seq=5#page_scan_tab_contents.

Baier, Annette. 2011. *The Pursuits of Philosophy: An Introduction to the Life and Thought of David Hume.* Cambridge, MA: Harvard University Press. Kindle edition.

Baker, Lee. 2018. *Correlation Is Not Causation.* Independently published.

Baker, Monya. 2016. "1,500 Scientists Lift the Lid on Reproducibility." *Nature* 533, 452–454. https://www.nature.com/articles/533452a.

Baker, Scott, Nicholas Bloom, Steven Davis, and Marco Sammon. 2021. "The Distinctive Character of Policy-Driven Stock Market Jumps." VOX EU, CEPR Policy Portal. May 21, 2021. https://voxeu.org/article/distinctive-character-policy-driven-stock-market-jumps.

Bambrough, Billy. 2021. "As Bitcoin's Total Value Nears $1 Trillion, These Crypto Prices Are Leaving Bitcoin in the Dust." *Forbes.* February 18, 2021. https://www.forbes.com/sites/billybambrough/2021/02/18/as-bitcoin-total-value-nears-1-trillion-these-crypto-prices-are-leaving-it-in-the-dust/?sh=25972a734689.

BBC News. 2008. "Study Shows How Spammers Cash In." *BBC News.* November 10, 2008. http://news.bbc.co.uk/2/hi/technology/7719281.stm.

Begley, C. Glenn, and Lee M. Ellis. 2012. "Raise Standards for Preclinical Cancer Research." *Nature* 483, 531–533. https://www.nature.com/articles/483531a.

Binmore, Ken. 2009. *Rational Decisions.* Princeton, NJ: Princeton University Press.

Blume, Stuart. 2017. *Immunization: How Vaccines Became Controversial.* London: Reakton Books Ltd.

Bodmer, Walter, R.A. Bailey, Brian Charlesworth, Adam Eyre-Walker,

Vernon Farewell, Andrew Mead, and Stephen Senn. 2021. "The Outstanding Scientist, R.A. Fisher: His Views on Eugenics and Race." *Heredity* 126, 565–576. https://www.nature.com/articles/s41437-020-00394-6.pdf.

Bogomolny, Alexander. 2020. *Cut the Knot*. Wolfram Media.

Brown, Matthew. 2021. "Poll: A Quarter of Americans Say Donald Trump Is 'True President' of the US." *USA Today*. May 25, 2021. https://www.usatoday.com/story/news/politics/2021/05/25/poll-quarter-americans-surveyed-say-trump-true-president/7426714002/.

Brunton, Finn. 2013. *SPAM: A Shadow History of the Internet*. Cambridge, MA: MIT Press.

Burkeman, Oliver. 2013. "Why the Spammers Are Winning." *The Guardian*. August 9, 2013. https://www.theguardian.com/technology/2013/aug/09/why-spammers-are-winning-junk-mail.

Burks, Barbara. 1928. "The Relative Influence of Nature and Nurture upon Mental Development; A Comparative Study of Foster Parent-Foster Child Resemblance and True Parent-True Child Resemblance." In: *The Twenty-Seventh Yearbook of the National Society for the Study of Education*, Barbara Burks et al. (eds.), 219–316. Bloomington, IL: Public School Publishing Company. https://www.gwern.net/docs/genetics/heritable/1928-burks-2.pdf.

Burks, Barbara et al. 1928. *The Twenty-Seventh Yearbook of the National Society for the Study of Education*. Bloomington, IL: Public School Publishing Company.

Burks, Barbara. 1932. "Needed Evidence." *American Society of Naturalists*. No. 710, 206–221. Reprint of paper read at Symposium on Heredity and Environment in Man. Atlantic City, December 30, 1932.

Burks, Barbara Stoddard, and Truman L. Kelley. 1928. "Chapter II: Statistical Hazards in Nature-Nurture Investigations." In: *The Twenty-Seventh Yearbook of the National Society for the Study of Education*, Barbara Burks et al.(eds.), 9–38. Bloomington, IL: Public School Publishing Company. https://www.gwern.net/docs/genetics/heritable/1928-burks-2.pdf.

Cardano, Girolamo. 2002. *The Book of My Life*. Translated by Jean Stoner, with an introduction by Anthony Grafton. New York: The New York Review Publishing.

Cardano, Girolamo. 2015. *The Book on Games of Chance*. Mineola, NY: Dover Publications.

Chen, Daniel L., Tobias J. Moskowitz, and Kelly Shue. 2016. "Decision Making Under the Gambler's Fallacy: Evidence from Asylum Judges, Loan Officers, and Baseball Umpires." *The Quarterly Journal of Economics* 131, no. 3 (August 2016), 1181–1242. https://academic.oup.com/qje/article/131/3/1181/2590011.

Chomsky, Noam. (2014). Science, Mind, and the Limits of Understanding. The Science and Faith Foundation, The Vatican. January 2014. https://chomsky.info/201401__/.

Clayton, Aubrey. 2021. *Bernoulli's Fallacy: Statistical Illogic and the Crisis of Modern Science*. New York: Columbia University Press.

Clifford, Catherine. 2017. "Bill Gates, Jeff Bezos and Warren Buffett have more wealth than half the population of the US combined." *CNBC Make It*. November 9, 2017. https://www.cnbc.com/2017/11/09/gates-bezos-buffett-have-more-wealth-than-half-the-us-combined.html.

Crockett, Zachary. 2016. "The Time Everyone 'Corrected' the World's Smartest Woman." Priceonomics. August 2, 2016. https://priceonomics.com/the-time-everyone-corrected-the-worlds-smartest/.

Cveticanin, Nikolina. 2021. "What's on the Other Side of Your Inbox—20 SPAM Statistics for 2021." DataProt. February 11, 2021. https://dataprot.net/statistics/spam-statistics.

Deacon, Terrence. 1998. *The Symbolic Species: The Co-evolution of Language and the Brain*. New York: W.W. Norton.

Deacon, Terrence. 2012. *Incomplete Nature: How Mind Emerged from Matter*. New York: W.W. Norton.

Dean, John. 2018. "Q&A with the Author: Prius or Pickup? How the Answers to Four Simple Questions Explain America's Great Divide." *Veridict Justia*. October 22, 2018. https://verdict.justia.com/2018/10/22/q-a-with-the-author-prius-or-pickup-how-the-answers-to-four-simple-questions-explain-americas-great-divide.

Dehouche, Nassim. 2021. "Revisiting the Volatility of Bitcoin with Approximate Entropy." *Cogent Economics and Finance* 10, Issue 1. https://www.tandfonline.com/doi/full/10.1080/23322039.2021.2013588.

Dejevsky, Mary. 2005. "Mary Dejevsky: Sir Roy Meadow Should Not Take All the Blame." *Independent*. July 14, 2005. https://www.independent.co.uk/voices/commentators/mary-dejevsky/mary-dejevsky-sir-roy-meadow-should-not-take-all-the-blame-298995.html.

Derman, Emanuel. 2012. *Models Behaving Badly*. New York: Free Press.

Derman, Emanuel, and Michael B. Miller. 2016. *The Volatility Smile*. New York: Wiley Finance.

Dimock, Michael, and Richard Wike. 2020. "America Is Exceptional in the Nature of Its Political Divide." Pew Research Center. November 13, 2020. https://www.pewresearch.org/fact-tank/2020/11/13/america-is-exceptional-in-the-nature-of-its-political-divide/.

Ditto, Peter H., Brittany S. Liu, Cory J. Clark, Sean P. Wojcik, Eric E. Chen, Rebecca H. Grady, Jared B. Celniker, and Joanne F. Zinger. 2019. "At Least Bias Is Bipartisan: A Meta-Analytic Comparison of Partisan Bias in Liberals and Conservatives." *Perspectives in Psychological Science* 14, No.2, 273–291. doi: 10.1177/1745691617746796.

Doll, Richard, and A. Bradford Hill. 1950. "Smoking and Carcinoma of the Lung." *British Medical Journal* 740, 739–748. https://www.ncbi.nlm.nih.gov/pmc/articles/PMC2038856/pdf/brmedj03566-0003.pdf.

Dowd, Kevin, John Cotter, Chris Humphrey, and Margaret Woods. 2008. "How Unlucky Is 25-Sigma?" ArXiv.org. March 24, 2008. https://arxiv.org/pdf/1103.5672.pdf.

Drexler, Madeline. 2002. *Secret Agents: The Menace of Emerging Infections*. Washington, DC: Joseph Henry Press.

Dsouza, Maxim. 2022. "Gambler's Fallacy—What It Is, Examples and Ways to Avoid." Productive Club. https://productiveclub.com/gamblers-fallacy/.

Dunnington, Guy Waldo. 1955. *Carl Friedrich Gauss: Titan of Science*. New York: Exposition Press.

Dyer, Owen. 2004. "Five Cases of Child Murder to Be Reopened." *BMJ* 328(7449), 1154. https://www.ncbi.nlm.nih.gov/pmc/articles/PMC411128/.

Eagleman, David. 2015. *The Brain: The Story of You*. New York: Vintage Books.

Earman, John. 1993. "Bayes, Hume, and Miracles." *Faith and Philosophy: Journal of the Society of Christian Philosophers* 10, no. 3, Article 1. https://place.asburyseminary.edu/cgi/viewcontent.cgi?article=1430&context=faithandphilosophy.

Economist. 2007. "Getting the Message, at Last: The Etiquette of Telecommunications." *The Economist*. December 13, 2007. https://www.economist.com/node/10286400/print?story_id=10286400.

Edwards, Griffith, ed. 2008. *Addiction: Evolution of a Specialist Field*. Hoboken, NJ: Wiley-Blackwell Publishing.

Egan, Matt. 2017. "Too-Big-to-Fail Banks Keep Getting Bigger." *CNN Business*. November 21, 2017. https://money.cnn.com/2017/11/21/investing/banks-too-big-to-fail-jpmorgan-bank-of-america/index.html.

Emma Email. 2020. "7 Words Sending Your Email to Spam." *Emma* (blog). https://content.myemma.com/blog/7-words-sending-your-email-to-spam.

Fanelli, Daniele. 2009. "How Many Scientists Fabricate and Falsify Research? A Systematic Review and Meta-Analysis of Survey Data." *PloS One* 4, no. 5, 35738. https://www.ncbi.nlm.nih.gov/pmc/articles/PMC2685008/.

Fazal, Tanisha, and Paul Poast. 2019. "War Is Not Over." *Foreign Affairs*. November/December 2019.

Fidler, Fiona, and John Wilcox. 2021. "Reproducibility of Scientific Results." *The Stanford Encyclopedia of Philosophy* (Summer 2021 edition), Edward N. Zalta (ed.). Section 2.2. https://plato.stanford.edu/entries/scientific-reproducibility/#MetaScieEstaMoniEvalReprCris.

Fierz, Markus. 1983. *Girolamo Cardano*. Boston: Birkhauser.

Fisher, R.A. [1925] 1973. *Statistical Methods for Research Workers*. New York: Hafner Publishing Company.

Fisher, R.A. 1930. "Inverse Probability." *Mathematical Proceedings of the Cambridge Philosophical Society* 26, 528–535. doi:10.1017/S0305004100016297.

Fisher, R.A. 1958a. "Cancer and Smoking." *Nature* 182. https://doi.org/10.1038/182596a0.

Fisher, R.A., 1958b. "Cigarettes, Cancer, and Statistics." *Centennial Review* 2, 151–166. https://www.york.ac.uk/depts/maths/histstat/fisher274.pdf.

Fisher, R.A., and W.A. Mackenzie. 2009. "Studies in Crop Variation. II. The Manurial Response of Different Potato Varieties." Published online by Cambridge University Press. March 27, 2009. https://doi.org/10.1017/S0021859600003592.

Frame, Paul. 2015. *Liberty's Apostle: Richard Price, His Life and Times*. Cardiff: University of Wales Press. Kindle version.

Galston, William A. 2021. "For COVID-19 Vaccinations, Party Affiliation Matters More Than Race and Ethnicity." Brookings. October 1, 2021. https://www.brookings.edu/blog/fixgov/2021/10/01/for-covid-19-vaccinations-party-affiliation-matters-more-than-race-and-ethnicity/.

Gauß, Carl Friedrich. 2022. *Letters of Carl Friedrich Gauß, 1777–1855*. Metadata and transcriptions by Menso Folkerts. Niedersächsische Staats- und Universitätsbibliothek Göttingen. Accessed February 8, 2022. https://gauss.adw-goe.de/handle/gauss/440.

Gimpel, James G., Nathan Lovin, Bryant Moy, and Andrew Reeves. 2020. "The Urban-Rural Gulf in American Political Behavior." *Political Behavior* (December). https://www.researchgate.net/publication/338607779_ The_Urban-Rural_Gulf_in_American_Political_Behavior/ download.

Goodman, Nelson. 1955. *Fact, Fiction, and Forecast*. Cambridge, MA: Harvard University Press.

Grafton, Anthony. 1999. *Cardano's Cosmos*. Cambridge, MA: Harvard University Press.

Grant, Adam. 2021. *Think Again*. New York: Penguin Random House.

Gumbel, E.J. [1958] 2004. *Statistics of Extremes*. Mineola, NY: Dover Publications.

Haigh, John. 1999. *Taking Chances*. Oxford: Oxford University Press.

Harris, James. 2015. *Hume: An Intellectual Biography*. Cambridge, UK: Cambridge University Press.

Hernán, Miguel A., and J.M. Robins. 2011. *Causal Inference: What If*. Boca Raton, FL: CRC Press.

Hester, Neil, and Kurt Gray. "For Black Men, Being Tall Increases Threat Stereotyping and Police Stops." 2018. Proceedings of the National Academy of Sciences of the United States of America 115, no. 11, 2711–2715. doi: 10.1073/pnas.1714454115.

Hoffman, Donald. 2019. *The Case Against Reality: Why Evolution Hid the Truth from Our Eyes*. New York: W.W. Norton.

Horgan, John. 2012. "What Thomas Kuhn Really Thought about Scientific 'Truth.'" *Scientific American*. May 23, 2012. https://blogs.scientificamerican.com/cross-check/ what-thomas-kuhn-really-thought-about-scientific-truth/.

Hume, David. 1739. *A Treatise of Human Nature*. Clarendon Press. https://oll.libertyfund.org/title/bigge-a-treatise-of-human-nature.

Hume, David. [1748] 2007. *An Enquiry concerning Human Understanding.* Edited with an introduction and notes by Peter Millican. New York: Oxford University Press.

Hume, David. 1776. *My Own Life.* https://www.econlib.org/book-chapters/chapter-my-own-life-by-david-hume/.

Hume, David. 1777. *Dialogues Concerning Natural Religion.* https://www.gutenberg.org/files/4583/4583-h/4583-h.htm#chap01.

Hume, David. 1789. *The History of England from the Invasion of Julius Caesar to the Revolution in 1688.* Volume 1. London: T. Cadell. https://archive.org/details/historyenglandf00humegoog/page/n29/mode/2up?view=theater.

Ioannidis, John P.A. 2005a. "Why Most Published Research Findings Are False." *PLOS Medicine* 2, no. 8, 124. https://upload.wikimedia.org/wikipedia/commons/8/8e/Ioannidis_%282005%29_Why_Most_Published_Research_Findings_Are_False.pdf.

Ioannidis, John P.A. 2005b. "Contradicted and Initially Stronger Effects in Highly Cited Clinical Research." *Journal of the American Medical Association* 294, no. 2, 218–228. doi:10.1001/jama.294.2.218.

Ioannidis, John P.A. 2008. "Why Most Discovered True Associations Are Inflated." *Epidemiology* 19, no. 5 (September), 640–648. https://med.mahidol.ac.th/ceb/sites/default/files/public/pdf/Repository/Why_Most_Discovered_True_Associations_Are_Inflated.2.pdf.

Johnson, Eric Michael. 2021. "Ronald Fisher Is Not Being 'Cancelled,' But His Eugenic Advocacy Should Have Consequences." *This View of Life.* April 12, 2021. https://thisviewoflife.com/ronald-fisher-is-not-being-cancelled-but-his-eugenic-advocacy-should-have-consequences/.

Kahn, Chris. 2020. "Americans Losing Faith in What Trump Says About the Coronavirus: Reuters/Ipsos Poll." *Reuters.* April 28, 2020. https://www.reuters.com/article/us-usa-election-poll/americans-losing-faith-in-what-trump-says-about-the-coronavirus-reuters-ipsos-poll-idUSKCN22A3CK.

Kahneman, Daniel, Olivier Sibony, and Cass R. Sunstein. 2021. *Noise: A Flaw in Human Judgment.* New York: Little, Brown Spark.

Kean, Sam. 2019. "Ronald Fisher, a Bad Cup of Tea, and the Birth of Modern Statistics." Science History Institute: Distillations. August 6, 2019. https://www.sciencehistory.org/distillations/ronald-fisher-a-bad-cup-of-tea-and-the-birth-of-modern-statistics.

Khovanova, Tanya. 2011. "Martin Gardner's Mistake." ArXiv.org. February 1, 2011. arXiv:1102.0173v1 [math.PR] 1 Feb 2011. https://arxiv.org/pdf/1102.0173v1.pdf.

King, D. Brett, Lizzi M. Montañez-Ramírez, and Michael Wertheimer. 1996. "Barbara Stoddard Burks: Pioneer Behavioral Geneticist and Humanitarian." In G.A. Kimble, C.A. Boneau, and M. Wertheimer (eds.), *Portraits of Pioneers in Psychology*, 2, 213–225. American Psychological Association. https://www.gwern.net/docs/genetics/heritable/1996-king.pdf.

Kirkegaard, Emil O.W. 2017. "Celebrating an Early Female Pioneer: Barbara Stoddard Burks." *Clear Language, Clear Mind* blog. March 24, 2017. https://emilkirkegaard.dk/en/2017/03/celebrating-an-early-female-pioneer-barbara-stoddard-burks/.

Klein, Ezra. 2020. *Why We're Polarized.* New York: Avid Reader Press.

Knight, Sam. 2009. "Is High IQ a Burden as Much as a Blessing?" *Financial Times.* April 10, 2009. https://www.ft.com/content/4add9230-23d5-11de-996a-00144feabdc0.

Knox, Dean, Will Lowe, and Jonathan Mummulo. 2020. "Administrative Records Mask Racially Biased Policing." *American Political Science Review*, 1–19. https://scholar.princeton.edu/sites/default/files/klm_full.pdf.

Koch, Christof. 2019. *The Feeling of Life Itself: Why Consciousness Is Widespread but Can't Be Computed.* Cambridge, MA: MIT Press.

Krauss, Alexander. 2018. "Why All Randomized Controlled Trials Produce Biased Results." *Annals of Medicine* 50, no. 4. https://www.tandfonline.com/doi/full/10.1080/07853890.2018.1453233.

Lehrer, Jonah. 2010. "The Truth Wears Off." *The New Yorker*. December 5, 2010. https://www.newyorker.com/magazine/2010/12/13/the-truth-wears-off.

Lexington Law. 2021. "Average Net Worth by Age for Americans." July 16, 2021. Lexington Law (blog). https://www.lexingtonlaw.com/blog/finance/average-net-worth-by-age.html.

Lienhard, John H., and Andrew Boyd. 2004. "No. 1950: Girolamo Cardano." Produced by John H. Lienhard. Podcast, 3:48, https://uh.edu/engines/epi1950.htm.

Lim, Milton. 2021. "Gauss, Least Squares, and the Missing Planet." Actuaries Digital. March 31, 2021. https://www.actuaries.digital/2021/03/31/gauss-least-squares-and-the-missing-planet/.

Lopez Museum and Library. 2012. "Sixteenth Century Artifact—Horoscope for the Birth of Jesus." December 29, 2012. https://lopezmuseum.wordpress.com/2012/12/29/twelve-days-of-christmas-day-4-sixteenth-century-artifact-horoscope-for-the-birth-of-jesus.

Maasoumi, Esfandiar, and Xi Wu. 2021. "Contrasting Cryptocurrencies with Other Assets: Full Distribution and the COVID Impact." August 25, 2021. https://economics.emory.edu/documents/maasoumi_wu_2021_jrfm_2021.pdf.

Mackenzie, Dana. 2018. "Barbara Stoddard Burks: Pioneer in Causality." Danamackenzie.com. March 1, 2018. http://danamackenzie.com/barbara-stoddard-burks-pioneer-in-causality/.

Magnet Academy. 2014. "Gauss-Weber Telegraph—1833." December 10, 2014. https://nationalmaglab.org/education/magnet-academy/history-of-electricity-magnetism/museum/gauss-weber-telegraph.

Mandelbrot, Benoit. 1963. "The Variation of Certain Speculative Prices." *The Journal of Business* 36, no. 4 (October 1963), 394–419. https://web.williams.edu/Mathematics/sjmiller/public_html/341Fa09/econ/Mandelbroit_VariationCertainSpeculativePrices.pdf.

Mandelbrot, Benoit, and Richard L. Hudson. 2007. *The Misbehavior of Markets*. New York: Basic Books.

Marchau, Vincent A.W.J., Warren E. Walker, Pieter J.T.M. Bloemen, and Steve W. Popper, eds. 2019. *Decision Making under Deep Uncertainty*. Springer. Open Access Publication.

Marche, Stephan. 2022. *The Next Civil War*. New York: Avid Reader Press.

McGraw, Meredith, and Sam Stein. 2021. "It's Been Exactly One Year Since Trump Suggested Injecting Bleach. We've Never Been the Same." *Politico*. April 23, 2021. https://www.politico.com/news/2021/04/23/trump-bleach-one-year-484399.

McGrayne, Sharon. 2011. *The Theory That Would Not Die: How Bayes' Rule Cracked the Enigma Code, Hunted Down Russian Submarines, and Emerged Triumphant from Two Centuries of Controversy*. New Haven, CT: Yale University Press.

McIntyre, Lee. 2018. *Post-Truth*. Cambridge, MA: MIT Press.

McNaughton, David. 2019. "Richard Price." *The Stanford Encyclopedia of Philosophy* (Winter 2019 edition), Edward N. Zalta (ed.). https://plato.stanford.edu/entries/richard-price/.

Meadow, Roy, ed. 1997. *ABC of Child Abuse*. 3rd edition. London: BMJ Publishing Group. https://archive.org/details/abcofchildabuse0000unse/mode/2up.

Mercier, Hugo. 2020. *Not Born Yesterday*. Princeton, NJ: Princeton University Press.

Miessler, Daniel. 2019. "Standard Deviations Explained." DanielMiessler.com. December 17, 2019. https://danielmiessler.com/blog/standard-deviations-explained/.

Mikulic, Matej. 2021. "Total Number of Registered Clinical Studies Worldwide Since 2000." Statista.com. September 21, 2021. https://www.statista.com/statistics/732997/number-of-registered-clinical-studies-worldwide/.

Mlodinow, Leonard. 2008. *The Drunkard's Walk: How Randomness Rules Our Lives*. New York: Pantheon Books.

Morin, David. 2016. *Probability: For the Enthusiastic Beginner.* CreateSpace.

Morris, Chris. 2021. "Jeff Bezos's Net Worth Falls by $13.5 Billion as Amazon Shares Sink." *Fortune.* July 30, 2021. https://fortune.com/2021/07/30/jeff-bezos-net-worth-amazon-stock-amzn-earnings-update/.

Morris, William Edward, and Charlotte R. Brown. 2019. "David Hume." *The Stanford Encyclopedia of Philosophy* (Spring 2021 edition), Edward N. Zalta, ed. Revised April 17, 2019. https://plato.stanford.edu/entries/hume/.

Mossner, Ernest. 2001. *The Life of David Hume.* 2nd edition. Oxford: Clarendon Press.

National Health Service. 2021. "Sudden Infant Death Syndrome (SIDS)." United Kingdom National Health Service. October 27, 2021. https://www.nhs.uk/conditions/sudden-infant-death-syndrome-sids/.

Noble, Kenneth B. 1995. "Prosecution Says Simpson Abused Wife for 17 Years." *The New York Times*, January 12, 1995. https://www.nytimes.com/1995/01/12/us/prosecution-says-simpson-abused-wife-for-17-years.html.

O'Connor, J.J., and E.F. Robertson. 2003. "Ronald Aylmer Fisher." MacTutor. Last updated October 2003. https://mathshistory.st-andrews.ac.uk/Biographies/Fisher/.

Offley, Ed. 1998. "The USS *Scorpion*—Mystery of the Deep: The Navy Says the Submarine's Sinking Was an Accident; Revelations Suggest a Darker Scenario." *Seattle Post-Intelligencer.* May 21, 1998. http://northwestvets.com/spurs/scorpion.htm.

Olson, Steve. 2004. "The Genius of the Unpredictable: The Man Who Invented Fractals Looks at the Stock Market, Math Education, and the Wild Improbability of His Own Life." *Yale Alumni Magazine.* November/December 2004. http://archives.yalealumnimagazine.com/issues/2004_11/mandelbrot.html.

Ore, Øystein. 1953. *Cardano: The Gambling Scholar*. Princeton, NJ: Princeton University Press.

Oxford Languages. 2022. "Word of the Year 2016." Oxford Languages. https://languages.oup.com/word-of-the-year/2016/.

Palosky, Craig. 2021. "Nearly a Quarter of Vaccinated Adults Received a COVID-19 Booster Shot, Up Sharply from October; Most Other Vaccinated Adults Expect to Get a Booster, Though About 1 in 5 Say They Likely Won't." KFF. December 2, 2021. https://www.kff.org/coronavirus-covid-19/press-release/nearly-a-quarter-of-vaccinated-adults-received-a-covid-19-booster-shot-up-sharply-from-october-most-other-vaccinated-adults-expect-to-get-a-booster-though-about-1-in-5-say-they-likely-wont/.

Pawar, Pritesh. 2022. "Why Do Spammers Misspell Words?" Priteshpawar.com. https://www.priteshpawar.com/why-do-spammers-misspell-words/cybersecurity/priteshpawar/.

Pearl, Judea, Madelyn Glymour, and Nicholas P. Jewell. 2016. *Causal Inference in Statistics: A Primer*. New York: Wiley.

Pearl, Judea, and Dana Mackenzie. 2018. *The Book of Why: The New Science of Cause and Effect*. New York: Hachette Books.

Phillips, Daniel. 2021. "How Many Bitcoin Does Its Inventor Satoshi Nakamoto Still Own?" Decrypt. January 3, 2021. https://decrypt.co/34810/how-many-bitcoin-does-its-inventor-satoshi-nakamoto-still-own.

Pinker, Steven. 2009. *How the Mind Works*. New York: W.W. Norton & Company.

Pinker, Steven. 2012. *The Better Angels of Our Nature: Why Violence Has Declined*. New York: Penguin Books.

Pinker, Steven. 2019. *Enlightenment Now: The Case for Reason, Science, Humanism, and Progress*. New York: Penguin Books.

Pinker, Steven. 2021. *Rationality*. New York: Viking.

Pishro-Nik, Hossein. 2014. "Introduction to Probability, Statistics, and Random Processes." Kappa Research.

Poitras, Geoffrey. 2011. "Richard Price, Miracles and the Origins of Bayesian Decision Theory." *The European Journal of the History of Economic Thought*, 20, no. 1. https://www.tandfonline.com/doi/10.1080/0 9672567.2011.565356.

Popper, Karl. 2002a. *Conjectures and Refutations: The Growth of Scientific Knowledge*. New York: Routledge.

Popper, Karl. 2002b. *The Logic of Scientific Discovery*. New York: Routledge.

Poundstone, William. 2019. *How to Predict Everything*. London: OneWorld Press.

Rao, C. Radhakrishna. 1992. "R.A. Fisher: The Founder of Modern Statistics." *Statistical Science* 7, no. 1 (February 1992), 34–48.

Rao, Justin M., and David H. Reiley. 2012. "The Economics of Spam." *Journal of Economic Perspectives* 26, no. 3, 87–110. https://pubs.aeaweb.org/doi/pdfplus/10.1257/jep.26.3.87.

Reference.com. 2020. "How Many People Are 7 Feet Tall?" April 8, 2020. https://www.reference.com/world-view/many-people-7-feet-tall-cb4f9973908981f1.

Reuters. 2020. "Fact Check: Clarifying the Comparison Between Popular Vote and Counties Won in the 2020 election." *Reuters*. December 29, 2020. https://www.reuters.com/article/uk-factcheck-votes-counties-election/fact-check-clarifying-the-comparison-between-popular-vote-and-counties-won-in-the-2020-election-idUSKBN2931UY.

Reuters. 2022. "Bitcoin Hovers Near More than 3-Month Lows after US Payrolls." *CNBC-TV18*. January 7, 2022. https://www.cnbctv18.com/cryptocurrency/bitcoin-hovers-near-more-than-3-month-lows-after-us-payrolls-12052772.htm.

River Financial. 2021. "How Much of the World's Money Is in Bitcoin?" River Financial. https://river.com/learn/how-much-worlds-money-in-bitcoin/.

Rizzo, Pete. 2021. "10 Years Ago Today, Bitcoin Creator Satoshi Nakamoto Sent His Final Message." *Forbes*. April 26, 2021. https://www.forbes.com/sites/peterizzo/2021/04/26/10-years-ago-today-bitcoin-creator-satoshi-nakamoto-sent-his-final-message/?sh=5e3b88bd10dd.

Rosenbaum, Paul. 2017. *Observation and Experiment*. Cambridge, MA: Harvard University Press.

Roser, Max, Joe Hasell, Bastian Herre, and Bobbie Macdonald. 2016. "War and Peace." OurWorldInData.org. https://ourworldindata.org/war-and-peace.

Ryssdal, Kai. 2018. "Panic, Fear and Regret: Conversation with Timothy Geithner, Ben Bernanke, and Henry Paulson." *Marketplace*, Minnesota Public Radio. https://features.marketplace.org/bernanke-paulson-geithner/.

Salsburg, David. 2001. *The Lady Tasting Tea: How Statistics Revolutionized Science in the Twentieth Century*. New York: W.H. Freeman.

Shakespeare, William. [1604] 2012. *Hamlet*. New York: Simon and Schuster Paperbacks.

Shearer, Elisa. 2021. "More Than Eight-in-Ten Americans Get News from Digital Devices." Pew Research Center. January 12, 2021. https://www.pewresearch.org/fact-tank/2021/01/12/more-than-eight-in-ten-americans-get-news-from-digital-devices/.

Shearer, Elisa, and Katerina Eva Matsa. 2018. "News Use Across Social Media Platforms 2018." Pew Research Center. September 10, 2018. https://www.pewresearch.org/journalism/2018/09/10/news-use-across-social-media-platforms-2018/#most-social-media-news-consumers-are-concerned-about-inaccuracy-but-many-still-see-benefits.

Silver, Nate. 2020. *The Signal and the Noise*. New York: Penguin Books.

Sjouwerman, Stu. 2022. "Here Is a Spam Message from 1864, as Old as the Victorian Internet." KnowBe4. May 30, 2022. https://blog.knowbe4.com/here-is-a-spam-message-from-1864-as-old-as-the-victorian-internet.

Skorupski, William P., and Howard Wainer. 2015. "The Bayesian Flip: Correcting the Prosecutor's Fallacy." *Significance* 12, no. 4 (August 2015). The Royal Statistical Society. https://rss.onlinelibrary.wiley.com/doi/full/10.1111/j.1740-9713.2015.00839.x.

Smith, Gary. 2017. *What the Luck?* New York: The Overlook Press.

Smith, Gary, and Jay Cordes. 2020. *The Phantom Pattern Problem: The Mirage of Big Data*. Oxford: Oxford University Press.

Smith, Gina. 2007. "Unsung Innovators: Gary Thuerk, the Father of Spam." *ComputerWorld*. December 3, 2007. https://www.computerworld.com/article/2539767/unsung-innovators--gary-thuerk--the-father-of-spam.html.

Stafford, Tom. "Why We Gamble like Monkeys." *BBC Future: Neurohacks*. January 27, 2015. https://www.bbc.com/future/article/20150127-why-we-gamble-like-monkeys.

Stanovich, Keith. 2021. *The Bias That Divides Us: The Science and Politics of Myside Thinking*. Cambridge, MA: MIT Press.

Stigler, Stephen. 1986. *The History of Statistics: The Measurement of Uncertainty before 1900*. Cambridge, MA: Belknap Press of Harvard University.

Stone, James. 2013. *Bayes' Rule*. Sheffield, UK: Sebtel Press.

Surgeon General's Advisory Committee on Smoking and Health. 1964. "Smoking and Health: Report of the Advisory Committee to the Surgeon General of the Public Health Service." United States, Public Health Service, Office of the Surgeon General. https://profiles.nlm.nih.gov/101584932X814.

Swift, Caleb. 2019. "Kurtosis and Bitcoin: A Quantitative Analysis." Hackernoon.com. September 7, 2019. https://hackernoon.com/kurtosis-and-bitcoin-uc55n3w5x.

Taleb, Nassim. 2001. *Fooled by Randomness: The Hidden Role of Chance in Life and in the Markets*. New York: Texere LLC.

Taleb, Nassim. 2007. *The Black Swan: The Impact of the Highly Improbable*. New York: Random House.

Taleb, Nassim. 2020. *Statistical Consequences of Fat Tails*. STEM Academic Press.

Toje, Asle. 2019. "The Causes of Peace: What We Know Now." Nobel Symposium Proceedings. Olso, Norway.

Trenholm, Richard. 2017. "Cold War Collision: US and Soviet Subs Crashed, CIA Files Reveal." *CNET*. January 25, 2017. https://www.cnet.com/news/cold-war-collision-us-and-soviet-subs-crashed-cia-memo-reveals/.

Trinity College Dublin. 2013. "Time Is in the Eye of the Beholder: Time Perception in Animals Depends on Their Pace of Life." *ScienceDaily*. September 16, 2013. https://www.sciencedaily.com/releases/2013/09/130916102006.htm.

Troy, Dave. 2016. "Is Population Density the Key to Understanding Voting Behavior?" Medium.com. August 22, 2016. https://davetroy.medium.com/is-population-density-the-key-to-understanding-voting-behavior-191acc302a2b.

University College London. 2022. "Ronald Aylmer Fisher (1890–1962)." UCL Centre for Computational Biology. https://www.ucl.ac.uk/biosciences/gee/ucl-centre-computational-biology/ronald-aylmer-fisher-1890-1962.

U.S. Census Bureau. 2002. "Table A-6: All Women and Currently Married Women of Reproductive Age (15–49 Years) by Region and Country: 1995–2025." In: *Global Population Profile: 2002*. https://www2.census.gov/programs-surveys/international-programs/tables/time-series/glob-pop-app-a/tab-06.pdf.

U.S. Census Bureau. 2011. "Table 205. Cumulative Percent Distribution of Population by Height and Sex: 2007 to 2008." In: *Statistical Abstract of the United States*, 135. https://www2.census.gov/library/publications/2010/compendia/statab/130ed/tables/11s0205.pdf.

Van Kessel, Patrick, and Dennis Quinn. 2020. "Both Republicans and Democrats Cite Masks as a Negative Effect of COVID-19, but for Very Different Reasons." Pew Research Center. October 29, 2020. https://www.pewresearch.org/fact-tank/2020/10/29/both-republicans-and-democrats-cite-masks-as-a-negative-effect-of-covid-19-but-for-very-different-reasons/

Wadman, Meredith. 2017. *The Vaccine Race.* New York: Penguin Books.

Weisberg, Herbert. 2014. *Willful Ignorance: The Mismeasure of Uncertainty.* Hoboken, NJ: John Wiley.

Wheeling, Kate. 2016. "Big Pharma Reveals a Biomedical Replication Crisis." *Pacific Standard.* Updated June 14, 2017. https://psmag.com/news/big-pharma-reveals-a-biomedical-replication-crisis.

Wilkinson, Will. 2019. "The Density Divide: Urbanization, Polarization, and Populist Backlash." Niskanen Center Research Paper. June 2019. https://www.niskanencenter.org/wp-content/uploads/2019/09/Wilkinson-Density-Divide-Final.pdf.

Woodworth, Robert S. 1943. "The Late Dr. Barbara Burks." June 7, 1943. *The New York Times.* https://timesmachine.nytimes.com/timesmachine/1943/06/07/96563336.html?pageNumber=12.

Worrall, John. 2020. "Popper and Kuhn on Theory Change." *Serious Science.* October 8, 2020. http://serious-science.org/popper-and-kuhn-on-theory-change-10268.

Yerushalmy, J. 2014. "The Relationship of Parents' Cigarette Smoking to Outcome of Pregnancy—Implications as to the Problem of Inferring Causation from Observed Associations." *International Journal of Epidemiology* 93, 1355–1366. doi: 10.1093/ije/dyu160.

Zilinsky, Jan, Jonathan Nagler, and Joshua Tucker. 2021. "Which Republicans Are Most Likely to Think the Election Was Stolen? Those Who Dislike Democrats and Don't Mind White Nationalists." *The Washington Post.* January 19, 2021. https://www.washingtonpost.com/politics/2021/01/19/which-republicans-think-election-was-stolen-those-who-hate-democrats-dont-mind-white-nationalists/.

Notes

Introduction

1. For this calculation, see Chapter 4.

Chapter 1

1. Background on Cardano is from Ore (1953), Fierz (1983), Mlodinow (2008), and Cardano's autobiography (2002).

2. Ore (1953), 12.

3. Ore (1953), 42.

4. Shakespeare ([1604] 2012), Act 3, Scene 1.

5. Ore (1953), 42.

6. Cardano (2002), *xx*.

7. Lopez Museum and Library (2012).

8. Near the end of his life, Cardano claimed he had published 131 books and burned 170 manuscripts, and that 111 books in manuscript form were still unpublished. Most of the books and manuscripts have been lost, but some were published posthumously in 1663, after the ban on his works by the Roman Catholic Church was lifted.

9. Al-Shawaf (2020).

10. Ore (1953), 52.

11. Ore (1953), 108.

12. Ore (1953), 109.

13. Crockett (2016).

14. Mlodinow (2008), 34.

15. See Knight (2009). for background on vos Savant.

16. Crockett (2016).

17. Mlodinow (2008), 34.

18. Crockett (2016).

19. Crockett (2016).

20. Crockett (2016).

21. Crockett (2016).

22. Knight (2009).

23. He was also an expert on Lewis Carroll, and his *The Annotated Alice* has sold more than a million copies.

24. Khovanova (2011). Gardner also asked a second question: "Mr. Jones has two children. The older child is a girl. What is the probability that both children are girls?" For ease of composition, I have dealt with that question as a follow-on to the discussion of Mr. Smith in the text.

25. The idea of this problem is from Morin (2016), 76.

26. This calculation and example are based on Morin (2016), 86.

27. I am assuming no twin, triplets, etc. and that birthdays are randomly distributed.

28. Cardano (2002), 189.

29. Stafford (2015).

30. Dsouza (2022).

31. Dsouza (2022).

32. This anecdote is based on Chen et al. (2016).

33. Chen et al. (2016), s.v. "V.A. Baseball Umpires: Data Description and Institutional Context."

34. Of these pitches, 30 percent were called strikes, and umpires made the right call 86 percent of the time.

35. Meadow (1997), 45.

36. McGrayne (2011), 262.

37. National Health Service (2021).

38. Dejevsky (2005).

39. Dyer (2004).

40. Noble (1995).

41. Skorupski and Wainer (2015).

42. Skorupski and Wainer (2015). Of course, this is based on convictions, and the actual number of murdered women is likely to be higher.

43. Skorupski and Wainer (2015) and U.S. Census Bureau (2002).

Chapter 2

1. Biographical details from Dunnington (1955).

2. Dunnington (1955), 13.

3. Magnet Academy (2014).

4. Dunnington (1955), 294.

5. Dunnington (1955), 239.

6. Dunnington (1955), 93.

7. Gauß (2022).

8. Dunnington (1955), 371.

9. Gauss's brain is still preserved at the department of physiology at the University of Göttingen.

10. The account of Ceres and Gauss is from Lim (2021).

11. Miessler (2019).

12. Reference.com (2020).

13. Reference.com (2020).

14. Reference.com (2020).

15. U.S. Census Bureau (2011).

16. Morris (2021).

17. Lexington Law (2021).

18. Clifford (2017).

19. Olson (2004).

20. Mandelbrot (1963).

21. Mandelbrot and Hudson (2007), 95.

22. Mandelbrot (1963), 394.

23. Mandelbrot and Hudson (2007), 167.

24. Taleb (2001), 102.

25. Taleb (2001), 102.

26. You could argue the fall in stock prices in early 2020 due to the COVID-19 pandemic was not a true black swan event because similar outbreaks, such as the Spanish flu of 1918, have occurred throughout history. On the other hand, pandemics are a type of black swan event, like a financial crisis, in which the cause varies by crisis. The Spanish flu was caused by an H1N1 virus crossing the species barrier from birds; the SARS-CoV-2 virus that causes COVID-19 is thought to be from a SARS virus in bats (or a Chinese lab). The financial crisis of 2008–2009 started with subprime mortgages; the 1987 crash was sparked by portfolio insurance. Clearly, black swans (the internet or Harry Potter books) and white swans (fires, floods) both exist. But some extreme events, such as pandemics, could be characterized as gray swans, with varying degrees of unpredictability.

27. Dowd et al. (2008), 1.

28. Dowd et al. (2008), 1.

29. Dowd et al. (2008), 6.

30. The following discussion is from Derman and Miller (2016), 144–160.

31. Each asset class has different volatility "smiles" or "smirks." For example, jumps in currency prices tend to be symmetrical, and so the implied volatilities of currency options exhibit more of a smile. As discussed, stock indexes jump down more often than up and thus have more of a smirk, with out-of-the-money put options priced more expensively than out-of-the-money call options. For a recent study of stock market jumps, see Baker et al. (2021).

32. In addition, there is a negative correlation between volatility and stock price movements. A significant piece of bad news typically generates greater uncertainty about the future; for example, the announcement of a declaration of war increases the expected variance of what could happen in the future. By contrast, stock markets tend to "melt up," as weeks and months of no significant news support stability and, hence, greater certainty about the days to come. Consequently, when prices move upward (or downward), the volatility map immediately shifts to a lower (or higher) level of overall volatility.

33. Mandelbrot and Hudson (2007), 248.

34. Two firms, the Bear Sterns Companies Inc. and Lehman Brothers Holdings Inc., actually did fail, but all other large banks were bailed out with taxpayer monies.

35. Egan (2017).

36. Egan (2017).

37. Egan (2017).

38. Ryssdal (2018).

39. Rizzo (2021).

40. Reuters (2022).

41. Phillips (2021).

42. Bambrough (2021).

43. River Financial (2021).

44. Maasoumi and Wu (2021).

45. Swift (2019).

46. Dehouche (2021).

47. Dehouche (2021).

48. When a cryptocurrency's underlying protocol is radically changed, this is called a "hard fork" because the blockchain splits into two paths: the previous protocol and the new protocol.

49. The hash rate is the unit used to measure the processing power of the bitcoin network.

50. Double-spending coins is paying two different users with the same bitcoins.

51. Pinker (2019), 451.

52. Roser et al. (2016), see National Defense Spending as a Percentage of GDP.

53. Roser et al. (2016); also see the chart, "International Battle Deaths per 100,000 People, 20th Century" by Acemoglu (2022).

54. Pinker (2012), 222.

55. Pinker (2012), 222.

56. Toje (2019), 75.

57. This may also be evidence that we are due for a major war soon.

58. Toje (2019), 35.

59. Fazal and Poast (2019), 76.

60. Fazal and Poast (2019), 75.

61. It is worth noting that if a global nuclear war had occurred there might not be anyone around to write or read about it. The fact that we are here may just be a consequence of survivor bias. Those wishing to pursue further, see my book *Fooled by the Winners*, Chapter 8, Nuclear War: Dumb Luck.

Chapter 3

1. Biographical details on Hume are from Baier (2011), Harris (2015), Mossner (2001), Hume (1776), and Morris and Brown (2019).

2. Hume (1777), Section 1, 1.

3. Morris and Brown (2019).

4. Mossner (2001), 5.

5. Mossner (2001), 30.

6. Hume (1776), 3.

7. Mossner (2001), 554.

8. Mossner (2001), 553.

9. Arkin (1995).

10. Baier (2011), Kindle edition, Location 44.

11. Mossner (2001), 231.

12. Hume (1776).

13. Hume (1776).

14. Hume (1789).

15. Goodman (1955), 59.

16. Goodman (1955), 59.

17. Goodman (1955), 66.

18. Goodman stated the problem differently by postulating that all emeralds are green and then turn blue after time t. But the basic idea is the same, and I think this formulation is more intuitive.

19. Goodman (1955), 82.

20. Goodman (1955), 83.

21. In his writings, Popper held that tolerance of the views of others, regardless of those views, was one of the most important foundations of an open society. Hence, he vehemently opposed all forms of authoritarianism. His position on this issue was, however, somewhat contradictory. Authoritarians advocate for intolerance. Using Popper's logic, we must tolerate the views of authoritarians who advocate for intolerance. Popper's beliefs in the virtues of tolerance were an outgrowth of his profound skepticism. If you are a true skeptic, then you should admit you cannot defend skepticism. A true believer in skepticism like Popper is not really a skeptic: they believe in skepticism as fervently as Christians believe in God. But at least the theist position is internally consistent. Skeptics need to pick a lane.

22. Popper (2002a), 42.

23. This partly explains the controversy Popper got himself into later in life when he defended creationism as a possible explanation for intelligent life, although he personally favored the theories of Darwin. It also accounts for his unwillingness to accept the position of atheists.

24. For an account of the discovery of Uranus, see Worrall (2020).

25. Worrall (2020) gives this example.

26. Horgan (2012), s.v. "The Structure of Thomas Kuhn."

27. Many of the ideas summarized in this section about human language are from Deacon (1998, 2012).

28. Pinker (2009), 73.

29. This idea and terminology concerning Kant comes from Hoffman (2019).

30. Hoffman (2019), 136.

31. Eagleman (2015), 63.

32. Hoffman (2019), 138.

33. Hoffman (2019), 138.

34. Trinity College Dublin (2013).

35. Trinity College Dublin (2013).

36. Trinity College Dublin (2013).

37. Koch (2019), 14.

38. Hoffman (2019), 42.

39. Hoffman (2019), 104.

40. Hoffman (2019), 81.

41. A study of how the idea-of-the-thing can change behavior is related to the physical features men find attractive in women. If asked, men will rarely express a strong preference for larger irises at the center of a woman's eyes. (They express other preferences with regard to size, but not this one.) However, when men were presented with two photos of a woman that were identical in all respects except the irises in one photo were slightly enlarged, men expressed a clear preference for the image with the larger irises. Larger irises offer a cue to reproduction: the size of a woman's irises, relative to the whites of the eye, declines with age; therefore, a larger iris indicates a younger woman, who is likely to be more fertile. In addition, some women's irises swell during ovulation. The men in the study chose the women they believed to be more attractive for reasons they did not understand. (Women and makeup companies probably figured this out a long time ago.) Evolution has tweaked men's brains to be attracted to images of larger irises. See Hoffman (2019) for a more complete discussion.

42. Chomsky (2014).

43. This may also explain why we struggle with quantum mechanics and the counter-intuitive notion that Schrödinger's cat, trapped in a steel box, can be both simultaneously dead and alive until we open the lid and peer inside and the cat wave collapses. Quantum mechanics has been repeatedly proven to be an accurate model of the subatomic world by physicists in the laboratory. But comprehending quantum entanglement has no evolutionary advantages when one is being chased by a saber-toothed tiger in the forest.

44. Hume [1748] (2007), Part IV, 31.

Chapter 4

1. Biographical background on Price is from Frame (2015) and McNaughton (2019).

2. Nonconformist or dissenting clergy were Protestant Christians who separated themselves from the state-sponsored Church of England because of disagreements over theological issues.

3. Frame (2015), Kindle version, location 513. "A lifetime of mercury"

refers to the use of mercury in the medicines used to treat venereal diseases at that time.

4. Frame (2015), Kindle version, location 513.

5. Frame (2015), Kindle version, location 801.

6. Poitras (2011).

7. Frame (2015), Kindle version, location 2746.

8. Hume [1748] (2007), Section X: Of Miracles.

9. Poitras (2011).

10. Earman (1993), 297.

11. Frame (2015), Kindle version, location 1054. Others propose calling it the Bayes-Price-Laplace theorem because the French mathematician Pierre-Simon Laplace also made significant improvements to Bayes's and Price's original ideas.

12. This account of Bayes's square table and two balls is from Stigler (1986), 182–190. Bayes expressed his formula in terms of continuous probabilities, and I have simplified the example to better illustrate his ideas.

13. Stigler (1986), 185.

14. Hester and Gray (2018).

15. Hester and Gray (2018).

16. Alternatively, probability squares work as well, but I think this "picture" is less clear than decision trees.

17. Trenholm (2017).

18. Offley (1998).

19. Offley (1998).

20. The account of Craven's search for the USS *Scorpion* is from McGrayne (2011), 196–205.

21. Cveticanin (2021).

22. See Burkeman (2013) for an account of the first spam.

23. Burkeman (2013).

24. Sjouwerman (2022).

25. *Economist* (2007).

26. Smith (2007).

27. Emma (2020).

28. Cveticanin (2021).

29. Cveticanin (2021).

30. Cveticanin (2021).

31. Rao and Reiley (2012).

32. BBC News (2008).

33. Pawar (2022).

Chapter 5

1. Biographical background on Fisher is from O'Connor and Robertson (2003), University College London (2022), and Bodmer et al. (2021).

2. Rao (1992), 47.

3. Bodmer et al. (2021), 568.

4. Bodmer et al. (2021), 568.

5. Bodmer et al. (2021), 569.

6.   Bodmer et al. (2021), 569.

7.   Bodmer et al. (2021), 571.

8.   Bodmer et al. (2021), 572.

9.   Johnson (2021).

10.   Johnson (2021) and Aldrich (2008).

11.   Bodmer et al. (2021), 565

12.   Fisher [1925] (1973), 9.

13.   Fisher (1930), 528.

14.   McGrayne (2011), 48.

15.   McGrayne (2011), 87.

16.   McGrayne (2011), 37.

17.   This example is from Pearl and Mackenzie (2018), 136.

18.   Pearl and Mackenzie (2018), 136.

19.   Background on a woman tasting tea is from Kean (2019) and Salsburg (2001).

20.   Fisher and Mackenzie (2008).

21.   Lehrer (2010).

22.   Lehrer (2010).

23.   Lehrer (2010).

24.   Krauss (2018).

25.   Krauss (2018), s.v. "Introduction."

26.   Krauss (2018), s.v. "Conclusions."

27.   Ioannidis (2005a), 0696.

28. Ioannidis (2005a), 0696.

29. Ioannidis (2005a), 0696.

30. Ioannidis (2005a), 0700–0701.

31. Ioannidis (2008), 641

32. Begley and Ellis (2012).

33. Begley and Ellis (2012).

34. Wheeling (2016).

35. Baker (2016).

36. Baker (2016).

37. Fanelli (2009).

38. Mikulic (2021).

39. Ioannidis (2005b).

40. Fidler and Wilcox (2021).

41. Fidler and Wilcox (2021).

42. Adler (2017).

Chapter 6

1. Background on Burks is from King et al. (1996).

2. Kirkegaard (2017).

3. L.M. Terman (1944), "Barbara Stoddard Burks, 1902–1943." *Psychological Review* 51, no. 2, 136–141, quoted in King et al. (1996).

4. J.H. Capshew and A.C. Laszlo (1986), "'We would not take no for an answer': Women Psychologists and Gender Politics during World War II." *Journal of Social Issues* 42, 157–180, quoted in King et al. (1996), 223.

5. Burks, quoted in King et al. (1996), 224.

6. Mackenzie (2018).

7. Woodworth (1943), 12.

8. Kirkegaard (2017).

9. I will refer to this as a causal diagram, but technically it is called a directed acyclic graph. See Burks et al. (1928), 12, for the actual diagram.

10. Burks (1928), 219.

11. This example is from Pearl and Mackenzie (2018), 141–143.

12. Pearl and Mackenzie (2018), 142.

13. Burks (1932), 210.

14. Kirkegaard (2017).

15. Burks (1928), 223.

16. Kirkegaard (2017); Burks and Kelley (1928), 20.

17. Burks (1932), 216.

18. Burks (1928), 32.

19. Burks (1932), 218.

20. This section is taken from Pearl and Mackenzie (2018), Chapter 5.

21. Surgeon General's Advisory Committee on Smoking and Health (1964).

22. Pearl and Mackenzie (2018), 169.

23. Pearl and Mackenzie (2018), 170.

24. Pearl and Mackenzie (2018), 170.

25. Pearl and Mackenzie (2018), 171.

26. Doll and Hill (1950), 742.

27.   Doll and Hill (1950), 745.

28.   Doll and Hill (1950), 744.

29.   Doll and Hill (1950), 744.

30.   Pearl and Mackenzie (2018), 174. The British Doctors' Study continued for more than fifty years and consistently demonstrated the causal link between smoking and lung cancer.

31.   Fisher (1958a), 596.

32.   Fisher (1958a), 596.

33.   Fisher (1958b), 163.

34.   Fisher (1958b), 163.

35.   Pearl and Mackenzie (2018), 174.

36.   Fisher (1958b), 155.

37.   Pearl and Mackenzie (2018), 225.

38.   Surgeon General's Advisory Committee on Smoking and Health (1964).

39.   This example is from Pearl and Mackenzie (2018), 183–185. The study was by Yerushalmy (2014).

40.   Yerushalmy (2014), 1361.

41.   Knox et al. (2020).

42.   Knox et al. (2020), 5. I have relabeled the letters in the causal diagram from the original paper for the sake of clarity.

43.   Knox et al. (2020), 12.

44.   Knox et al. (2020), 14.

45.   Knox et al. (2020), 14.

46.   Knox et al. (2020), 17.

Chapter 7

1. Dimock and Wike (2020).

2. Galston (2021).

3. Palosky (2021).

4. Van Kessel and Quinn (2020).

5. Van Kessel and Quinn (2020).

6. Van Kessel and Quinn (2020).

7. Stanovich (2021), 140.

8. Stanovich (2012), 140.

9. Stanovich (2021), 140.

10. Alesina et al. (2020), 327.

11. Alesina et al. (2020), 327.

12. Brown (2021).

13. Zilinsky et al. (2021).

14. Alesina et al. (2020), 324.

15. For an excellent recent book about confirmation or myside bias, see Stanovich (2021).

16. We may get a second opinion. But that will also be from an expert.

17. Stanovich (2021), 56.

18. Stanovich (2021), 56.

19. Stanovich (2021), 57 and 61.

20. Stanovich (2021), 71 and 120.

21. Shearer (2021).

22.   Shearer (2021).

23.   McIntyre (2018), 51.

24.   McIntyre (2018), 51.

25.   Shearer (2021).

26.   Acemoglu et al. (2022), 22.

27.   Acemoglu et al. (2022) is a good example of one of these studies.

28.   Allred (2018).

29.   Shearer and Matsa (2018).

30.   McIntyre (2018), 62.

31.   Gimpel et al. (2020), 14.

32.   Troy (2016).

33.   Wilkinson (2019).

34.   Wilkinson (2019).

35.   Reuters (2020).

36.   Klein (2020), 38.

37.   Klein (2020), 38.

38.   McIntrye (2018), 12.

39.   Oxford Languages (2022).

40.   Ditto et al. (2019).

41.   McGraw and Stein (2021).

42.   Kahn (2020).

Index

Goodman, Nelson, 60–62, 200n18
Google, 162

H

Halibut (submarine), 94
Hall, Monty, 11–12, 27
hard fork, 47, 198n48
Herschel, William, 64
Hill, Austin, 137–140
Hoffman, Donald, 73
Homo sapiens
 evolution, 2, 169
 eyes of, 71
 perceive color, 71
hot streaks, 20, 22, 23
Huchthausen, Peter, 95
Hume, David, 53–54, 79, 102, 155
 and Adam Smith, 53–55
 and American independence, 54
 arguments on atheism, refused by
  price, 80–82
 and critics, 55
 *Dialogues Concerning Natural
  Religion*, 75
 existence of God, arguments
  against, 75–76
 family of, 54
 "Of Miracles," 80
 personal life of, 54
 problem of induction, 56–60
 A Treatise of Human Nature, 53, 56
The Hunt for Red October (Clancy), 94

I

IBE. *See* inference to the best
  explanation
"idea-of-the-thing," 70–72, 73,
  202n41
induction, 53–56, 67, 81
 and critical rationalism, 62, 63
 formulation of, 58, 60–62

inductive justification of, 59
 solution to, 59
inference to the best explanation
  (IBE), 58
Institute for Genetic Biology and
  Racial Hygiene, 105
intelligence, 133–135
inverse probability, 81–83, 108
 in height and racial prejudice,
  84–85
Ioannidis, John, 118

J

Jaggers, Joseph, 21
Jefferson, Thomas, 78
Johnson, Lyndon B., 96
JPMorgan, 43, 44
Jung, Carl, 126

K

K-129 (submarine), use of Bayes' theo-
  rem to search, 94–95
Kant, Immanuel, 70
 The Critique of Pure Reason, 79
Katrina (Hurricane), 39
Khovanova, Tanya, 194n24
Kuhn, Thomas, 64–66
 and Popper, 66
 scientific revolutions to evolution,
  66
 *The Structure of Scientific Revolu-
  tions*, 64

L

"law of large numbers," 19, 20, 27,
  34, 35
Leibniz, Gottfried, 9

About the Author

DAVID LOCKWOOD is a former lecturer on the faculty of the Graduate School of Business at Stanford University. He has three decades of experience as a senior executive in Silicon Valley and has served on more than twenty public and private company boards. In addition, he has been a senior advisor to the US government on nuclear and energy issues.